W9-ADI-351

WONDERS OF ITALY

A Photographic Journey through Landscape, Art, and Architecture

FABRIZIA VILLA

METRO BOOKS
New York

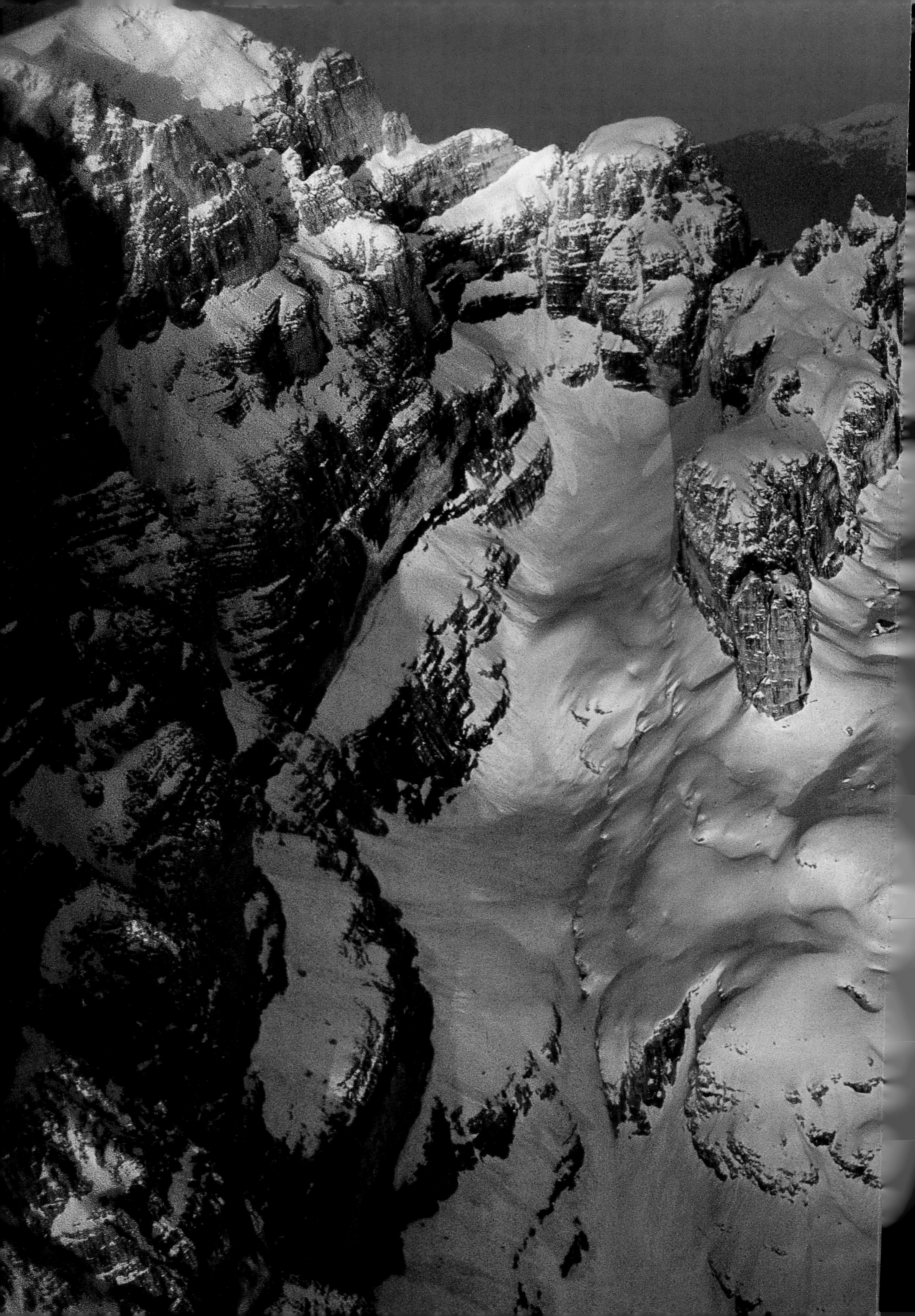

Contents

Introduction

"Wonder is the sudden surprise of the soul which makes it tend to consider attentively those objects which seem to it rare and extraordinary," wrote Descartes in his moral treatise *The Passions of the Soul*. Before Descartes, Plato and Aristotle had maintained that wonder lies at the origin of human desire to obtain knowledge. So perhaps it is this very response of wonderment and awe to the extraordinary treasures of Italy that has attracted travelers over the centuries.

There are so many examples of natural, aesthetic, archaeological, and architectural beauty on the Italian peninsula. The wonders in this book provoke the same feelings of amazement and the desire to explore as in Jules Verne's *Around the World in 80 Days*; they also serve as a microcosm for Italy's eventful history and colorful theater of human experience. We have therefore focused on specific aspects of each city, town, artistic work, or building, in an attempt to capture the essential human spirit that makes each a wonder in its own right. Our journey takes us through a country that, like no other in western Europe, has made a virtue of diversity, having preserved—since it is such a young state, unified a mere 150 years ago—a huge wealth of different regional identities, heritage, languages, cuisines, traditions, and architectural styles, all of which make the Italy of today truly wonderful.

Thanks to its ancient history and the power of the Roman Empire, when Italy was at the very heart of the expanding Western civilization, it is now home to the world's greatest cultural heritage, with more than 3,400 museums, over 40 UNESCO World Heritage Sites, and some 2,100 archaeological parks and sites. To select just 80 wonders from among this huge number was virtually an impossible task. We have sought to create a "museum of the imagination" that embraces all aspects of the Italian character, a virtual, visual puzzle that, when pieced together through its different eras, encompasses the true identity of the country, linking the ancient and the modern, nature and architecture, language and art.

Our aim is to reconstruct the history of Italy's artistic heritage and culture, from the colorful scenes inside the tombs at Tarquinia, to the wall paintings at Pompeii, and the frescoes of Giotto, Michelangelo, and Raphael. Exploring a series of magical places, including the Valley of the Temples in Agrigento and Hadrian's Villa at Tivoli, we chart the development of sculpture, continuing our journey through Tuscany, where sculpture and architecture combined in the building of magnificent cathedrals. Tuscany is also where two of the greatest sculptures of the Renaissance were created, Donatello's *David* around 1430, and some 70 years later, Michelangelo's *David*. We encounter Michelangelo's work again, this time in the Sistine Chapel and in St. Peter's in Rome, just a few steps from the stunning Raphael Rooms in the Vatican Museums. The genius of these great artists still astounds the viewer today, as does Leonardo's work in Milan. Our journey continues thanks to the great patrons of the history of Italian art and architecture, who made wonder their raison d'être and without whom it would not be possible to construct our museum of the imagination today: Emperor Hadrian, Ludovico the Moor, Ercole I d'Este, Federico da Montefeltro, Cosimo de' Medici, Federico Gonzaga, Scipione Borghese, Charles III of Spain, and Federico Borromeo. Nor must we forget the great papal patrons—Julius II, Leo X, and Innocent X—for whom art was a way of exercising power and who left behind priceless treasures throughout the Italian peninsula, a reflection of their own brilliant and enlightened minds.

Today, just as in the past, we also admire Italy's natural wonders, where charming villages integrate so perfectly in the rich and varied landscape. Just a short walk or drive takes travelers from one environment to another, often differing dramatically, from the majestic panoramas and dizzying heights of the Alps and the Dolomites, to the beautiful lakes, where architecture and landscape combine in idyllic scenes. We pass through verdant cultivated farmlands, such as in the Langhe in Piedmont, and in the Val d'Orcia and the Crete Senesi in Tuscany, not such distant neighbors but so different from each other. The journey continues offshore, through the wild charm of the islands, from the volcanic Aeolian Islands in the Scicilian Archipelago, to the less rugged Capri and Ponza. The sense of wonder, the sudden surprise of the soul of which Descartes spoke, casts its spell once more, in magical places where man has left his indelible mark, such as the Sassi di Matera or the rural landscape of the Itria Valley, a beautiful patchwork of *trulli* and olive trees.

In this grand tour for the soul, there's an open dialogue between the traveler and each stone and monument, every landscape and work of art. Visitors to Italy continue to be amazed by the country's great heritage, and the vital sense of wonder that is the source of knowledge that here, as in no other place, remains undiminished.

2-3 *The majestic mountain range of the Brenta Dolomites is protected by UNESCO.*

4-5 *The small colorful houses of Manarola in the Cinque Terre face the tiny harbor.*

6-7 *An early morning mist hovers over the fields in Val d'Orcia.*

9 *Filippo Lippi's* Coronation of the Virgin *decorates the half cupola of the apse in Spoleto Cathedral.*

10-11 *One of the Dionysian-themed frescoes decorating the* triclinium *(dining room) of the Villa dei Misteri ("Villa of the Mysteries") in Pompeii.*

16-17 *A masterpiece of the Pisan Romanesque and focus of the Piazza dei Miracoli, Pisa's Cathedral of Santa Maria Assunta is flanked by the famous tower.*

18-19 *A baroque masterpiece, Gian Lorenzo Bernini's s sculptural group of* Apollo and Daphne *is at the Galleria Borghese in Rome.*

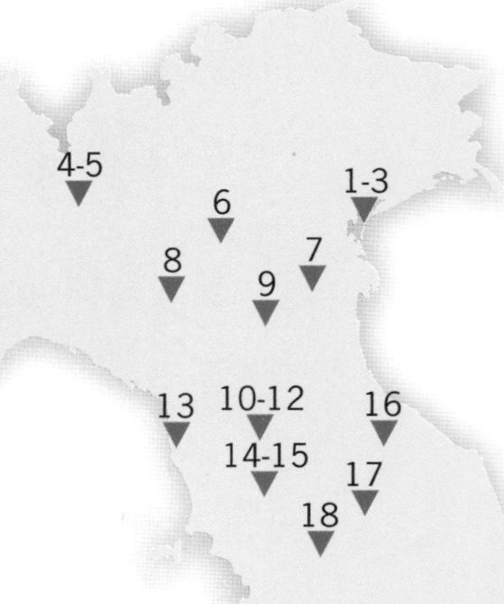

▼ARCHITECTURE

▼ART

For the chapter on art, the works are arranged chronologically rather than geographically, as for all the other chapters.

Landscapes and Villages: Italy's Great Natural Theater page 162

Archaeology: The Roots of History page 232

ARCHAEOLOGY

LANDSCAPE

Architecture: A Phenomenon of the Emotions

Sometimes, looking at what is on the outside helps us to better observe ourselves inside. This is what happens, for example, in Peter Greenaway's film The Belly of an Architect, *a hymn to the architecture of the Eternal City, where the importance of each individual's destiny is dwarfed by the ancient stones of Rome, a common feeling when confronted by the magnificent buildings that make Italian cities unique. Bearing this in mind and the words of Le Corbusier, the father of modern architecture, "Architecture is a thing of art, a phenomenon of the emotions," in this book we cross the Italian peninsula from north to south via its architectural wonders, to be held spellbound by the most famous of its monuments. These great collective works—the majestic cathedrals, castles, palaces of noblemen, the squares, and bridges—were built and subsequently transformed over the centuries in the wake of the historical events that affected each locality. If today, it is an individual architect who designs a structure, the buildings of the past were, in comparison, collective works, vast constructions sites in which Italian artists labored together for centuries. Take, for example, St. Mark's Basilica in Venice, enriched over time with precious works of art from distant places such as Constantinople, or the Cathedral of Monreale, which the Normans designed as a true architectural melting pot. Or St. Peter's Basilica, a construction site for 120 years, which saw the services of no fewer than seven site foremen, whose names alone embrace a wide sweep of the history of Italian architecture between the Renaissance and the baroque, and from Bramante to Raphael, from Michelangelo to Bernini. Not only that, art and architecture have often operated in pairs, supporting each other in mutual fashion. Thus were born the masterpieces of Romanesque and Gothic architecture, which saw the ablest painters and sculptors of the times at work in the great cathedrals, such as Nicola Pisano and his son Giovanni, who were engaged first in Pisa to work on the baptistery and the cathedral, then later in Siena, to sculpt the cathedral's pulpit, and then later still in Perugia, where father and son decorated what is the oldest public fountain still in existence, the Fontana Maggiore, with its celebrated bas-reliefs. One of Nicola Pisano's pupils, Arnolfo di Cambio, was responsible for some of Italy's superb medieval buildings, such as the Cathedral of Orvieto, a masterpiece on whose facade more than 20 artists worked over the centuries. Its current Gothic form was the work of Lorenzo Maitani of Siena, its glittering interior the perfect home for the frescoes of Fra Angelico and of Luca Signorelli, painted in the 15th century. The Cathedral of Santa Maria del Fiore in Florence is linked in particular with Tuscan architect and sculptor Arnolfo di Cambio, who designed and worked on the cathedral. He was succeeded by Giotto, who took over as foreman, dealing specifically with the cathedral's bell tower, one of the showpieces of Italian architecture. The tower, which almost looks as if it was created in paint, became one of the greatest sculptors' workshops of the 1300s, beginning with Donatello. At the start of the 15th*

century, the Cathedral of Santa Maria del Fiore astounded the entire world, with its large unreinforced dome designed by Brunelleschi, who proved that design could overcome construction problems, transforming him from head foreman into architect. And it was in fact Brunelleschi who, with Leon Battista Alberti, marked the birth of the Renaissance architecture that would go on to develop throughout the 15th and 16th centuries, enriching the entire Italian peninsula with sublime works of art and buildings, thanks also to the patronage of families like the Medicis in Florence, the Gonzagas in Mantua, the Estes in Ferrara, and the Viscontis and Sforzas in Milan. And so the court artist and architect was born, a development that was also of interest for Rome, once the papal residence had returned there after being installed in Avignon, in France, for some 70 years. Every city was transformed in its own way to reflect the grandeur of its lords, such as Federico da Montefeltro, who in Urbino erected that "palace in the form of a city," a utopia made reality as a result of the work of three architects, Luciano Laurana of Dalmatia, Maso di Bartolomeo, and Francesco di Giorgio Martini of Siena. It was Biagio Rossetti who, in the 15th century, brought to fruition the vision of Ercole I d'Este by creating in Ferrara the first great example of modern town planning, the so-called Herculean Addition, which doubled the size of the city, propelling it from the Middle Ages into the Renaissance. An eclectic artist, like many others of the Renaissance, he was responsible for another superb building designed to enhance life at court, this time in Mantua. It was to Giulio Romano, capable of designing "not dwellings for men but homes for the gods," to whom Federico II Gonzaga entrusted his dream—the Palazzo Te, the renowned Mannerist villa designed as the duke's pleasure palace. The Renaissance even left its mark on buildings that were already in existence, built in previous eras. The castle in Milan is a good example, where Francesco Sforza rebuilt it on the foundation of the Viscontis' medieval palace-fortress, adding a clock tower with a portal beneath, designed by Filarete, in the facade facing the city. The work was continued by Sforza's sons Galeazzo Maria and Ludovico the Moor, who transformed the castle into a stately residence, thanks also to the contributions of artists like Bramante and Leonardo da Vinci. Things were also changing toward the south, albeit in a different way, where the dominance of the Spanish Aragons in Naples led to Castel dell'Ovo being enriched as a royal palace; the towers were lowered and the defensive structures reinforced. It was under the Bourbon kings of Naples that architectural splendor reached its apotheosis in southern Italy. In the 1700s, Charles III of Spain (Charles VII of Naples), commissioned the Royal Palace at Caserta, an Italian-style Versailles designed by the great architect Luigi Vanvitelli. An interpreter of European classicist tendencies, he created his most important work here, illustrating, once again, the words of Le Corbusier, "The purpose of construction is to make things hold together; of architecture to move us."

St. Mark's: East Meets West in a Design Masterpiece

VENICE

What goes around, comes around, you might say, following the adventures of the four splendid horses in the Triumphal Quadriga of St. Mark's Basilica in Venice. In 1798, the year after the fall of the Venetian Republic, the gigantic gilded bronze sculptures symbolic of the Venetian basilica were taken by Napoleon to Paris, where they remained until 1815, before being reinstated on the gallery in the facade looking out over Piazza San Marco. The prancing horses were looted as war booty from Constantinople by Eric Dandolo in 1204, after the Fourth Crusade—the year the city was sacked—and were taken to Venice, along with other priceless works. Some experts attribute their creation to Roman sculptors working under Constantine the Great, while others believe them to be of ancient Greek origin. The basilica was constructed in 828 to house the remains of Saint Mark, which had been stolen from Alexandria in Egypt, and was subsequently rebuilt, beginning in 1063, on a Greek-cross plan, with five hemispherical domes of obvious Byzantine inspiration. This encounter with Oriental style produced a distortion in the church's architecture. The domes were raised and covered with sheets of lead to be clearly visible from the sea, but the entire exterior of the building was transformed quite radically. The great arches of the facade were clad with marble; and columns, capitals, sculptures, and entire marble structures from the Orient were installed in the brick facades. "La Serenissima" was at the peak of its splendor at this time, and St. Mark's and the Doge's Palace were the city's glittering symbols. It was also around this time that the interior of the basilica was covered with gilded mosaics, lending it an unprecedented fluidity and harmony. Depicting stories from the Old and New Testaments, the mosaics cover more than 86,111 square feet (8,000 square meters) of walls, vaults, and cupolas: a biblical history in images that unifies the basilica's interior space, flooding it with a heavenly, burnished light. The floors, also of Byzantine inspiration, are laid with polychrome marble mosaics in geometric designs, although more muted in color than the wall decorations that cover 22,593 square feet (2,099 square meters).

22 *Beside St. Mark's Basilica, St. Mark's Campanile (bell tower) soars to a height of 325 feet (99 meters). The current building is an exact reproduction of the bell tower that collapsed in 1902. From the belfry a view of the whole of Venice can be enjoyed.*

23 *Throughout the centuries, the majestic Basilica of St. Mark has reflected the Venetian Republic's power and wealth. The Venetians have helped to make it a masterpiece by introducing works of art from all over the world.*

BENEDITUSQUIUENITINNOMINEDOMINI

24 Depicting the descent of the Holy Spirit onto the Apostles as rays of light, the mosaics in the Pentecost cupola are among the oldest (12th century) of the five cupolas in St. Mark's.

25 The mosaic work in the atrium of St. Mark's Basilica illustrates the events related in the Pentateuch, such as the story of Noah and the Great Flood, which can be seen to one side of the main portal.

26-27 Until 1850, the Rialto Bridge was the only one to cross the Grand Canal. The present stone bridge was designed in 1591 by Antonio da Ponte, who won a competition in which Andrea Palladio also competeted.

27 The Ca' d'Oro ("Golden House"), with its characteristic facade combining Gothic and Oriental elements, owes its name to the gilding that once adorned the front. Today it is home to the Galleria Giorgio Franchetti museum.

The Seductive Charms of the Grand Canal

VENICE

Venice has had to adapt itself to the reversed S shape of the Grand Canal since its very beginning, spreading out along its shores and following in the wake of its meandering progress. The Canalasso, as the Venetians call it, divides the city into two parts, each with three districts or *sestieri*—with those located on one side of the canal referred to as "*de Citra*" and those on the other side as "*de Ultra*"—and the two sides connected by four bridges. In 2008, the Ponte della Costituzione, designed by Spanish architect Santiago Calatrava, joined the three other historical bridges: the Ponte degli Scalzi, the Ponte dell'Accademia, and the Ponte di Rialto or famous Rialto Bridge. Originally, the great sweep of water leading from Piazzale Roma to the San Marco basin was simply the channel through which goods passed on their way to the storehouse-homes of wealthy Venetian merchants. Then, in 1591, with the rebuilding of the Ponte di Rialto in stone—it was previously made of wood and opened for passing boats—it became an iconic thoroughfare. Between the 15th and 18th centuries, over 170 residences were built along the canal shoreline, enriching it with their Gothic, Renaissance, and baroque facades that, reflected along the 2.4 miles (3.8 kilometers) of water, still today recount the stylistic evolution of the architecture of Venice. No one arriving in the lagoon at the Santa Lucia railway station can help but be amazed. As soon as you get off the train, you are plunged into the past, beginning with the dome of San Simeone Piccolo, one of the few churches facing onto the Grand Canal. Then, from the *vaporetto* (the public water bus), you can enjoy the incredible parade of noble palaces, starting with the Byzantine-style Fondaco dei Turchi, now home to the Museo di Storia Naturale di Venezia, one of the many museums along the Grand Canal (including the Ca' Pesaro, housing the Galleria Internazionale d'Arte Moderna and the Museo d'Arte Orientale); the Ca' d'Oro or "Golden House"; Palazzo Grassi, which holds the François Pinault Collection of contemporary art; and the Ca' Rezzonico on the other side of the canal, which hosts the Museo del Settecento. Farther along, you come to the Palazzo Venier dei Leoni, housing the Peggy Guggenheim Collection, and the 17th-century Punta della Dogana, supporting Palazzo Grassi since 2009 as a home to the François Pinault Collection. The triangular area of land from which the dome of the Basilica of Santa Maria della Salute rises marks the beginning of the division of the Grand Canal from the Giudecca Canal, while on the opposite bank, the waters of the Canalasso fade into those of the San Marco basin.

The Imposing Doge's Palace

VENICE

Powerful on land and powerful on sea, *Mars* and *Neptune*, the huge statues sculpted by Sansovino in the second half of the 16th century, bear witness to the supremacy of "La Serenissima" (as Venice was known) at the top of the Giants' Staircase ("Scala dei Giganti"), which was named after them. This area symbolizes the grandeur of the Republic of Venice more powerfully than any other, with the Doge's Palace ("Palazzo Ducale"), an imposing Gothic building that overlooks the grandiose Piazza San Marco. It was at the top of this spectacular staircase that the newly elected Doge, the Republic's highest authority, received his ceremonial headgear (the *corno ducale*) and swore to uphold the constitution during a ceremony that has been depicted in all its magnificence by the greatest of the Venetian landscape painters, particularly Guardi and Canaletto. What can be seen of the palace today—facades of pink and white marble surmounting a loggia with interlaced arches above the portico—is the result of renovation. Originally conceived as a fortress, construction began around 1340 to meet the need to house, not 400, but 1,200 individuals eligible to participate in the legislative assembly, known as the Grand Council ("Maggior Consiglio"). This wing, toward the basin of San Marco, is the oldest in the palace and hosts the immense Hall of the Grand Council ("Sala del Maggior Consiglio"), 174 feet (53 meters) long and 79 feet (24 meters) wide. Voting on new laws was held here and great feasts were organized, with a capacity of up to 3,000 people. Two of the great masterpieces of the Doge's Palace, Tintoretto's *Paradise*, nearly 30 feet (9 meters) high, and Veronese's *Apotheosis of Venice*, are also to be found here, along with portraits of 77 of the Doges. The splendor of Venice continues to impress as you make your way round the palace's other imposing institutional chambers and the Doge's apartments, but takes on a darker aspect in the terrible New Prisons, connected by the famous Bridge of Sighs with the Magistrato alle Leggi Chamber ("Sala del Magistrato alle Leggi") and the Quarantia Criminal Chamber ("Sala della Quarantia Criminal"). The statues and reliefs decorating the exterior of the building are no less precious than those inside, turning the Doge's Palace into a comprehensive catalog of sculpture. Indeed, all the exterior capitals are sculpted with allegorical and religious motifs, ranging from the Vices and Virtues to the Months of the Year, and from the Zodiac to the Judgment of King Solomon.

28 *The corners of the Doge's Palace are decorated with reliefs showing the Drunkenness of Noah (here, with the Bridge of Sighs in the background), Adam and Eve (between the square and the Molo, or quay), and The Judgment of Solomon (near the Porta della Carta).*

28-29 *Dominated by the slender shape of the bell tower, St. Mark's Square is Venice's civic and religious heart. At its perimeter rise the domes of St. Mark's and the stunning Gothic facade of the Doge's Palace.*

30-31 *A painting by Francesco Bassano on the walls of the Hall of the Grand Council shows the doge receiving the papal sword from Pope Alexander III before setting sail with the fleet against Barbarossa.*

31 *The Hall of the Grand Council is in the palace wing, facing St. Mark's Basin. In addition to Veronese's Apotheosis of Venice and Tintoretto's Paradise, 77 portraits of the doges can be seen here.*

The Soaring Spires of the Cathedral

MILAN

The cathedral's heart beats in time to the rhythm of the city, as becomes clear when you climb up to its roof terraces, the unforgettable location for the heartbreaking scene in the film *Rocco and His Brothers* by Luchino Visconti. From 230 feet (70 meters) up, surrounded by spires, pinnacles, flying buttresses, and statues of saints, you can take in a view of the whole of Milan, a city whose expansion the cathedral has watched over since 1386. Today, the skyscrapers of the Porta Nuova and Repubblica Garibaldi districts, created for Expo 2015, have joined the historic landmarks of the castle, the Torre Velasca, and the Pirelli Tower. In preparation for this event, new restoration work has begun on the Duomo, Milan's symbolic cathedral, so its spires may continue to soar in all their glory. A typical feature of Gothic architecture, the spires are some of the most perfect examples. The Duomo has a forest of 135 spires 56 feet (17 meters) high, adorned with a wealth of ornamentation and statues of every shape and size, made from the Candoglia marble that Gian Galeazzo Visconti made available to the Veneranda Fabbrica (Venerable Factory of the Duomo of Milan, responsible for its construction and maintenance) for the building of the cathedral that brought him prestige throughout Europe. The cathedral's worksite was possibly the first truly European construction site in history. Over the course of 20 years, foreign engineers, architects, sculptors, and stonecutters arrived in Milan to join the local workers and bring their knowledge of the Gothic architecture of Central Europe. From the very beginning, sculpture played an important role in this and continued to develop without interruption for six centuries. In total, 3,400 statues and 700 figures feature in high relief, adorning the facade, the vaults, the spires, and the stained glass windows. There is a host of saints and prophets, culminating in the *Madonnina*, a golden statue of the Virgin Mary, which has towered over the Duomo's main spire at a height of 356 feet (108.5 meters) since 1774. The cathedral interior features five naves, divided by 52 enormous pillars that support the vaults and contains 55 stained glass windows. These masterpieces in glass play their role in instructional preaching, representing an authentic "Bible for the poor," the most striking example of which is the impressive central window dedicated to the Revelation.

33 *Milan's Duomo is the only Gothic cathedral that can boast such a large number of spires. They surround the lantern, forming a crown around the main spire, on which a gilded statuette of the Virgin stands.*

34-35 The composite facade of the Milan Cathedral began to take shape in 1590, under the direction of architect Pellegrini. It was continued in the 17th century by Richini and Buzzi, finally reaching completion in the 19th century.

35 The crypt or Coro Jemale was designed by architect Pellegrino Pellegrini beneath the main altar. Circular in shape, the choir surrounds a central altar for the relics.

The Life and Times of the Castello Sforzesco

MILAN

In a way, the history of the Castello Sforzesco ("Sforza Castle") begins at its end, in the years between the Unification of Italy and the beginning of the 20th century. It was only then, in fact, that the fortress constructed in the 15th century on the orders of Francesco Sforza, on the foundations of the former castle built by the Visconti family, took on its current name and appearance. Architect Luca Beltrami was responsible for the task of restoring and rebuilding the complex, and in so doing of repairing the relationship between the citizenry and its manor. The castle was accordingly restored to the people of Milan and was used to house museums and art collections, including the Museo d'Arte Antica ("Museum of Ancient Art"), where you can see the famous *Rondanini Pietà* by Michelangelo. Culminating in 1905 with the inauguration of the Torre del Filarete, which had been struck by lightning in 1521 and never rebuilt, the restoration work finally healed the wounds inflicted on the building over the centuries by the various ruling houses. The Torre del Filarete—the tower over the castle entranceway—was originally erected by Francesco Sforza to enhance the castle facade that looked toward the city, a first step in the fortress's transformation into a ducal manor, which began in 1466 with work ordered by Sforza's sons, Galeazzo Maria and Ludovico, Il Moro. Galeazzo Maria commissioned the Corte Ducale ("Ducal Courtyard"), flanked by La Rocchetta, the castle stronghold, with an elegant Renaissance portico, and another tower, the Torre di Bona. Ludovico succeeded in attracting the most important artists of the era to Milan, from Bramante, to whom La Ponticella is attributed, the small covered bridge crossing the outer moat, to Leonardo, who painted the incredible pergola on the ceiling of the Sala delle Asse ("Room of the Wooden Panels"), and Bramantino, who painted his Argo fresco in the Sala del Tesoro ("Treasury"). Ludovico was ousted from power, and after some two decades of French rule, Ludovico's son Francesco II Sforza took over. He proved to be the last duke of Milan, his death marking the end of the castle's role as ducal mansion. It was at this point that the building that had previously been labeled "the stronghold of tyranny" began its most challenging period, several centuries during which it was transformed into a large barracks for Spanish, French, and lastly, Austrian troops, until the year 1848 and the Five Days of Milan, the rebellion that forced the Austrians from the city and, shortly afterward, the ambitious reconstruction of Luca Beltrami.

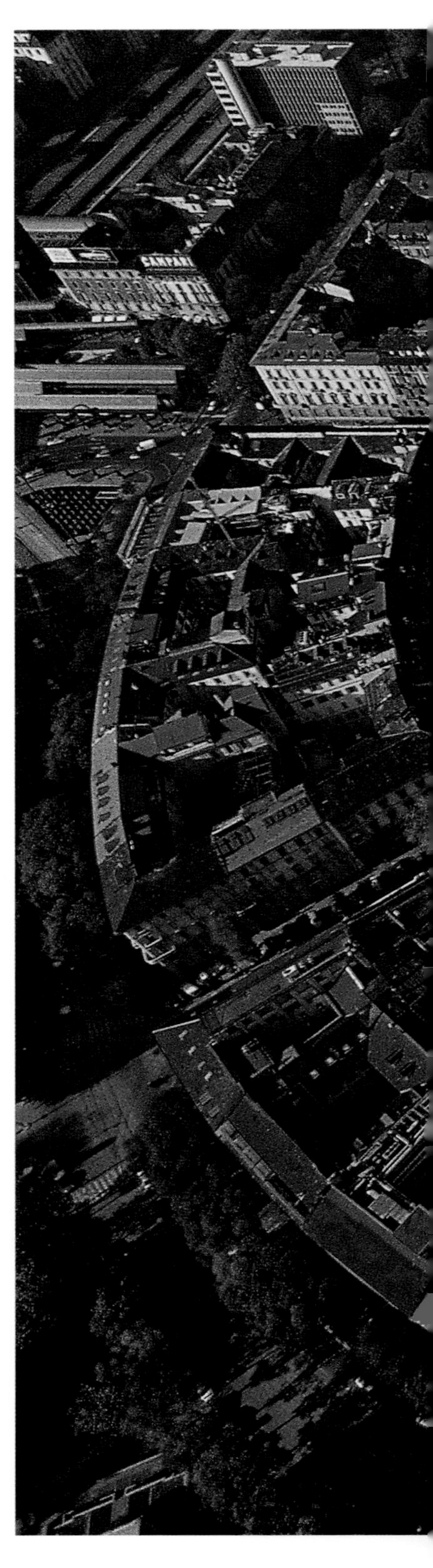

36 Galeazzo Maria commissioned the Ducal Chapel ("Cappella Ducale"), which was decorated by painters such as Bonifacio Bembo, Giacomino Vismara, and Stefano de Fedeli. A choir assembled from all over Europe gathered to sing here.

36-37 The current appearance of the Castello Sforzesco dates back to the urban renewal that took place after the Unification of Italy and, in particular, to the restoration work carried out by architect Luca Beltrami, which began in 1893.

The Art of Leisure at Palazzo Te

MANTUA

Gossip was a serious matter in Mantua in the 1500s, and even more so when it concerned the duke, to the extent that it was spread across the palace walls. The theme of the frescoes in the Chamber of Amor and Psyche is in essence a pictorial metaphor for the unhappy love affair between Federico II Gonzaga and the beautiful Isabella Boschetti. The frescoes, inspired by the tales of Apuleius and other love stories from mythology, were painted by Giulio Romano, Raphael's favorite pupil, who was summoned to Mantua by the duke to build a palace "for the honorable leisure of the prince, for him to restore his strength in tranquility." Initially, Gonzaga requested that the painter and architect simply refurbish the existing stables to "organize a little space where he could go and have lunch once in a while, or a leisurely dinner," but seeing the quality of Giulio Romano's work on the frescoes, Frederico entrusted the artist with an even greater commission, the sumptuous Palazzo Te, a masterpiece that would represent the pinnacle of Romano's ingenuity as an architect. Situated just outside the city's defensive walls, the building is square in shape with a large inner courtyard, the Courtyard of Honor, with the duke's rooms laid out on the ground floor. For the exterior of the palace, Romano drew upon the classical tradition, combining the Doric style with the naturalism typical of Mannerism. However, it is in the frescoes and stuccos in the interior that his work truly reaches the sublime. In his decorations of the palace rooms, depicting mythological, biblical, and astrological subjects, Romano reveals the influence of his former master Raphael, but also the power of Michelangelo, as revealed in the compelling Chamber of the Giants ("*Camera dei Giganti*"), where the mythological rebellion of the Titans is illustrated across the walls and vault, a pictorial play for which those who view it are the audience. In the Hall of the Horses ("*Sala dei cavalli*"), dedicated to the great passion of the Gonzaga family, the illusion continues with the life-sized depictions of favorite horses against a backdrop painted to resemble marble columns; the gaze of Morel Favorito, Glorioso, Dario, and Battaglia seems to follow visitors as they move around the hall, the largest in Palazzo Te.

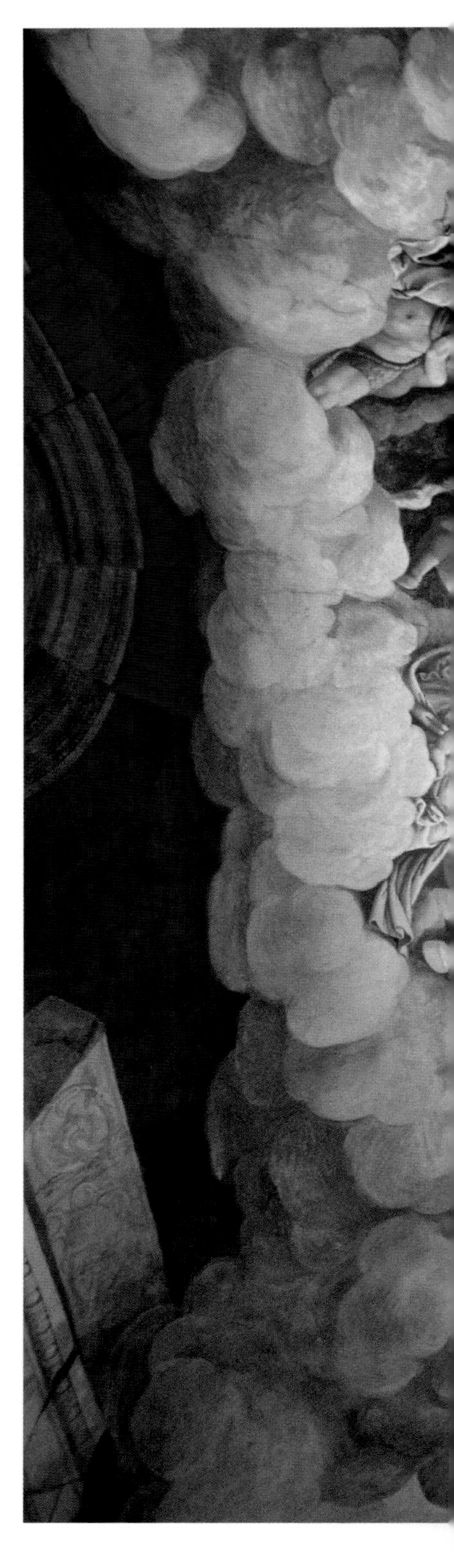

38 Palazzo Te, intended for the amusement and recreation of the lords of Mantua, is designed around the Courtyard of Honor ("Cortile d'Onore"). The exterior is decorated in typical Mannerist style.

38-39 The Chamber of the Giants ("Sala dei Giganti"), showing the rebellion of the Titans as they are surprised by Jupiter, is considered Giulio Romano's masterpiece. He built and decorated Palazzo Te between 1525 and 1535 for Federico II Gonzaga.

40-41 *Designed for hosting banquets and dinners for illustrious guests, the Chamber of Amor and Psyche ("Sala di Amore e Psiche") is the most sumptuous in the Palazzo Te. Here Giulio Romano cleverly blends eros and myth, taking inspiration from Apuleius.*

41 *On the south and west walls of the Chamber of Amor and Psyche, Giulio Romano shows the preparations for a sumptuous banquet prepared for the gods on the Isle of Venus, ideally compared with the Island of Te.*

Hotel Ferrara

The Labors of Hercules

FERRARA

"A superstar ahead of his time" is a fitting description for Biagio Rossetti, the architect who interpreted the vision of Ercole I d'Este, duke of Ferrara, in the 15th century, leaving to history the first great example of modern town planning. The Herculean Addition, as the urban plan was called and which has remained almost unchanged to this day, doubled the size of Ferrara at a stroke, delivering a layout based on a grid system, with straight roads intersecting at right angles. The city was thus catapulted out of the Middle Ages—the quarter south of the Viale Cavour and Corso Giovecca in today's city still retains its medieval character—and into the Renaissance—the north of the modern-day city, with its wider, straighter streets and new churches and buildings, including the remarkable Palazzo dei Diamanti exemplifies this style. Designed by Rossetti himself, the palace derived its name from its cladding of marble blocks carved in the shape of diamonds. Since 1992 the palace has played host to some superb art exhibitions, which have both placed the city at the heart of the Italian cultural scene and given it a second Renaissance. Surrounded by almost 6 miles (9 kilometers) of walls that are among the best preserved on the Italian peninsula, the focal point of the city, in the wake of the Herculean Addition, is the Castello Estense, a castle with square towers in each corner and surrounded by a water-filled moat. Constructed in 1385 for defensive purposes, it later evolved, under Ercole I, into the duke's aristocratic residence. In the 15th century, the fortress was connected to the Palazzo Municipale, or City Hall, the first residence of the Este family. In front stands the supreme symbol of the medieval city, Ferrara cathedral, dedicated to San Giorgio in 1135, its Romanesque and Gothic elements combining harmoniously on its tripartite facade. The bell tower, built in the mid-15th century, was designed in the Renaissance style by Leon Battista Alberti. The Palazzo Schifanoia was also built for the ducal family and is the only one of the so-called *Delizie Estense* that can be visited in the city. The "Estense delights" were designed for the family's entertainment and leisure use. Built in 1385 and then modified in 1493 under Biagio Rossetti, the palace is famous for its celebrated cycle of frescoes representing the twelve months of the year. For this masterpiece Borso d'Este brought together the most distinguished artists of Ferrara, such as Francesco del Cossa and Ercole de' Roberti.

42-43 THE CASTELLO ESTENSE, BUILT IN 1385, WAS TRANSFORMED IN THE 15TH CENTURY WHEN THE MILITARY FORTRESS BECAME THE RESIDENCE OF DUKE ERCOLE I D'ESTE, WHO DOUBLED THE DIMENSIONS OF THE BUILDING BETWEEN THE TORRE MARCHESANA (ALSO KNOWN AS THE CLOCK TOWER) AND THE TORRE DEI LEONI ("LION'S TOWER").

43 THE TRIPARTITE FACADE OF FERRARA CATHEDRAL, BEGUN IN 1135, BLENDS ROMANESQUE AND GOTHIC ELEMENTS. TO THE SIDE OF THE CATHEDRAL IS THE LOGGIA DEI MERCIAI, USED AS A STOREHOUSE AND WORKSHOP SINCE THE MIDDLE AGES.

44 The Triumph of Minerva is one of the scenes painted by Francesco del Cossa on the east wall of the Hall of the Months ("Salone dei Mesi") in the Palazzo Schifanoia, commissioned by Borso d'Este, to highlight his position as duke.

45 The Month of April was painted on the east wall by Francesco del Cossa, depicting the Triumph of Venus. The iconographic program was developed by court astrologer and librarian Pellegrino Prisciani.

The Middle Ages on Display

PARMA

Looking up at the cupola over the chancel in the Cathedral of Santa Maria Assunta in Parma, you have the strange and unsettling sensation of falling upward. Painted between 1526 and 1530 by Antonio Allegri, known as Correggio, the *Assumption* of the Virgin draws the viewer toward the divine light. The Virgin rises to heaven, surrounded by a host of saints, angels, cherubs, and musicians, as her Son, bathed in a dazzling light, comes to meet her. The dizzying *Assumption* is at the heart of the imposing cathedral, acknowledged as one of the highest examples of Po Valley Romanesque and the hub of Piazza Duomo, the cathedral square around which the medieval city grew up. Competing with Correggio's fresco for the role of "star of the show," a high-relief by Benedetto Antelami, on the wall of the right transept, depicts the deposed Christ. Sculpted around 1178, some 20 years before the construction of the Baptistery, the *Deposition* marked the artist's first steps toward a taste for the Gothic, an early departure from the rigorous sobriety of the Lombard-Emilian Romanesque style. But in the red marble relief carved for cathedral, all the elements of the figurative art can be seen, upon which Antelami, as both sculptor and architect, subsequently drew for his designs for the Baptistery. For the decoration of the building, based on an octagonal plan, Antelami made reference both to the Romanesque and Byzantine traditions and, above all, to French Gothic. The vertical structure and the sense of rhythm are Gothic, punctuated by three portals with architraves and lunettes sculpted with themes alluding to the salvation of humanity through baptism, while inside, the lunettes portray scenes from the Bible. Nevertheless, Antelami reached the pinnacle of sculptural art with his cycle of the Months, Seasons, and related Zodiacal Signs, a calendar of allegorical sculptures representing a perfect synthesis of classical and Gothic influences in the artist's work.

46 Work on the cathedral began around 1059 outside the city walls, upon a preexisting Paleo-Christian basilica. It was consecrated in 1106 by Pope Paschal II, who went to Parma in the retinue of Matilda of Canossa.

47 Piazza Duomo is the religious nucleus of Parma, the square around which the medieval city proceeded to develop. The Cathedral of Santa Maria Assunta, the Baptistery, and the Bishop's Palace all face onto it.

48 TOP *BENEDETTO ANTELAMI'S LUNETTES OVER THE PORTALS INSIDE THE BAPTISTERY PORTRAY SCENES FROM THE OLD TESTAMENT, SUCH AS THE PRESENTATION AT THE TEMPLE (SHOWN HERE), THE FLIGHT INTO EGYPT, AND KING DAVID PLAYING THE HARP.*

48 BOTTOM *THE FRESCO ON THE VAULT IN THE BAPTISTERY IS DIVIDED INTO HORIZONTAL BANDS OF IMAGES. THE FIRST ILLUSTRATES SCENES FROM THE LIFE OF ABRAHAM; THE SECOND, THE LIFE OF JOHN THE BAPTIST; THE THIRD CONTAINS PORTRAYALS OF THE PROPHETS; AND THE FOURTH, THE APOSTLES.*

49 *DESIGNED BY ANTELAMI BETWEEN 1196 AND 1216, THE VAULT OF THE OCTAGONAL BAPTISTERY IS DIVIDED BY 16 STONE RIBS SUPPORTED ON COLUMNS. EACH OF THE TRIANGULAR SPACES FORMED ABOVE CONTAINS A PAINTED SCENE.*

50-51 *Bologna's two towers, the Asinelli Tower and the Garisenda Tower, with the copper dome of the nearby Church of San Bartolomeo e Gaetano, emerge from the center of the sea of red roofs in Italy's Emilia-Romagna region.*

51 *The Asinelli Tower was erected in 1119 to add luster to the Ghibelline family name. From the top of its 498 steps, completed in 1684, you can enjoy the best panoramic view of the city.*

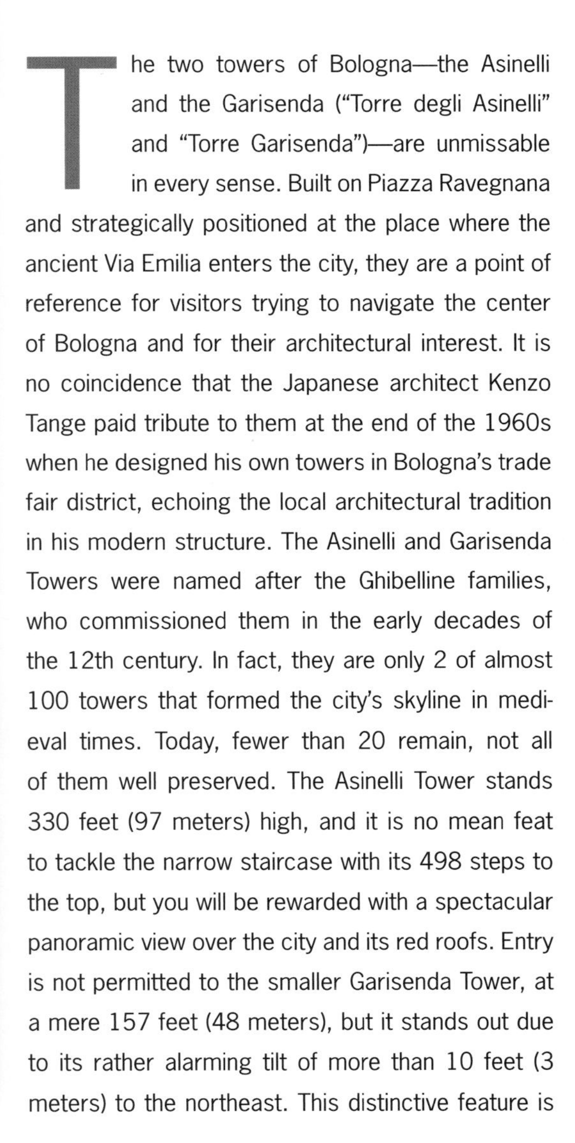

A City Bows to its Imposing Towers

BOLOGNA

The two towers of Bologna—the Asinelli and the Garisenda ("Torre degli Asinelli" and "Torre Garisenda")—are unmissable in every sense. Built on Piazza Ravegnana and strategically positioned at the place where the ancient Via Emilia enters the city, they are a point of reference for visitors trying to navigate the center of Bologna and for their architectural interest. It is no coincidence that the Japanese architect Kenzo Tange paid tribute to them at the end of the 1960s when he designed his own towers in Bologna's trade fair district, echoing the local architectural tradition in his modern structure. The Asinelli and Garisenda Towers were named after the Ghibelline families, who commissioned them in the early decades of the 12th century. In fact, they are only 2 of almost 100 towers that formed the city's skyline in medieval times. Today, fewer than 20 remain, not all of them well preserved. The Asinelli Tower stands 330 feet (97 meters) high, and it is no mean feat to tackle the narrow staircase with its 498 steps to the top, but you will be rewarded with a spectacular panoramic view over the city and its red roofs. Entry is not permitted to the smaller Garisenda Tower, at a mere 157 feet (48 meters), but it stands out due to its rather alarming tilt of more than 10 feet (3 meters) to the northeast. This distinctive feature is due to subsidence of the soil and led the poet Dante Alighieri, in *Divine Comedy* (*Inferno*, Canto 31), to compare the giant Antaeus, as he bent down from above in order to lower him into the abyss of Caina, with the tower of Garisenda. In more recent times, the towers have been immortalized in a three-dimensional animation created for the virtual theater at Palazzo Pepoli, the 18th-century building that has housed the new Museo della Storia di Bologna since 2012. The focus of the renovation project for the building, which was designed by architect Mario Bellini, is another tower, known as the "Tower of Time." The glass and steel structure erected over the building's courtyard links the rooms and floors of the museum, in which tribute is paid to the history of the two towers that symbolize the city.

52-53 AND 53 *The cathedral's name, Santa Maria del Fiore, is said to refer to the lily, the symbol of the city of Florence. Construction began in 1296 and concluded only in 1887, with the completion of the facade.*

The Duomo: A Glorious Architectural Feat

FLORENCE

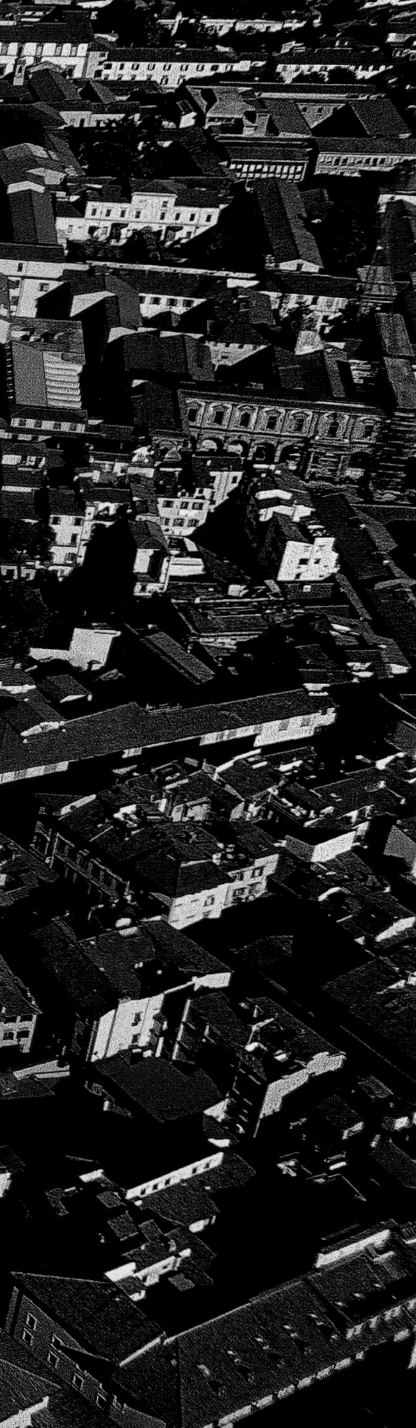

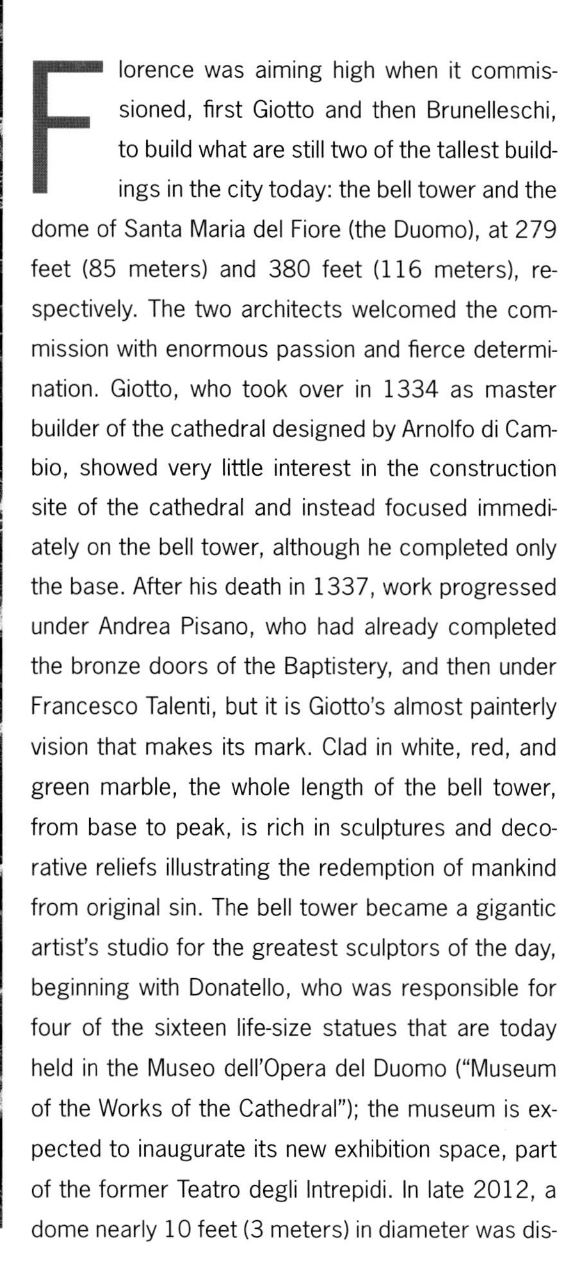

Florence was aiming high when it commissioned, first Giotto and then Brunelleschi, to build what are still two of the tallest buildings in the city today: the bell tower and the dome of Santa Maria del Fiore (the Duomo), at 279 feet (85 meters) and 380 feet (116 meters), respectively. The two architects welcomed the commission with enormous passion and fierce determination. Giotto, who took over in 1334 as master builder of the cathedral designed by Arnolfo di Cambio, showed very little interest in the construction site of the cathedral and instead focused immediately on the bell tower, although he completed only the base. After his death in 1337, work progressed under Andrea Pisano, who had already completed the bronze doors of the Baptistery, and then under Francesco Talenti, but it is Giotto's almost painterly vision that makes its mark. Clad in white, red, and green marble, the whole length of the bell tower, from base to peak, is rich in sculptures and decorative reliefs illustrating the redemption of mankind from original sin. The bell tower became a gigantic artist's studio for the greatest sculptors of the day, beginning with Donatello, who was responsible for four of the sixteen life-size statues that are today held in the Museo dell'Opera del Duomo ("Museum of the Works of the Cathedral"); the museum is expected to inaugurate its new exhibition space, part of the former Teatro degli Intrepidi. In late 2012, a dome nearly 10 feet (3 meters) in diameter was discovered in the construction site for the new museum, with bricks arranged in a herringbone pattern, the same technique as that used by Brunelleschi to construct the cupola for the Duomo. This was the greatest challenge the architect had to face, and it was thanks to careful observation of ancient monuments that he managed to execute what appeared to be an impossible task. Between 1418 and 1434, Brunelleschi succeeded in building the cathedral's dome—more than 148 feet (45 meters) in diameter—without using support beams, in so doing providing his successors with one of the largest surface areas ever to be frescoed: 38,750 square feet (3,600 square meters), which were decorated by Vasari and Zuccari in the Cinquecento, the Italian Renaissance of the 16th century. With the cupola for the Duomo, Brunelleschi established the primacy of design over construction, and from that point onward, the role of the architect would never again be confused with that of a mere foreman.

ECCE.HOMO
I·N·R·I

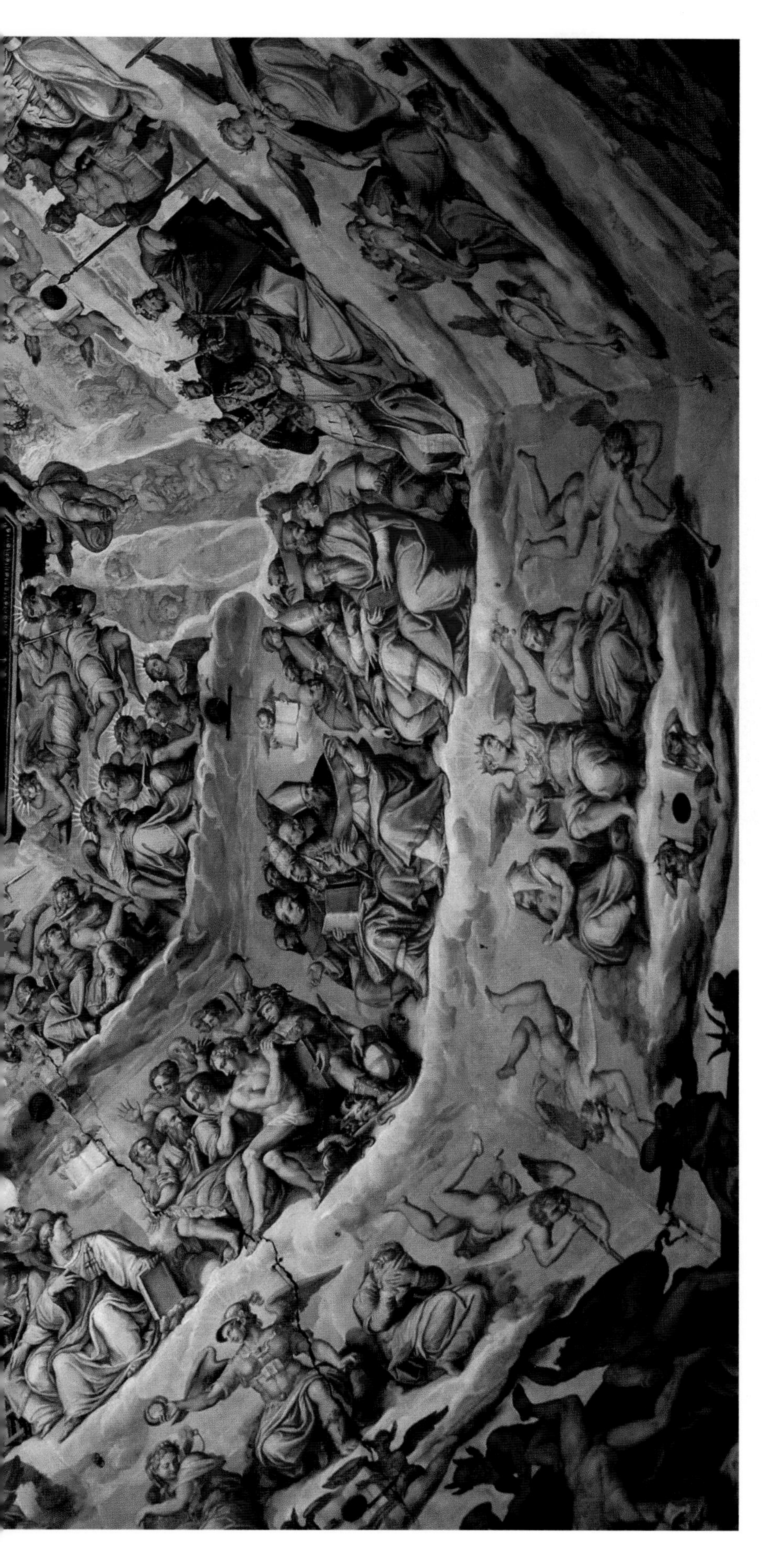

54-55 *The fresco of the Last Judgment inside the cathedral dome is by Giorgio Vasari and Federico Zuccari. Brunelleschi's masterpiece, the dome was erected without reinforcement by making use of a double-shell design (an inner and outer dome) separated by a gap of several feet inside which the dome's structural ribs and struts were concealed.*

The Piazza della Signoria: A Witness to History

FLORENCE

The Piazza della Signoria was born out of hatred—the hatred between the Guelphs and the Ghibellines, the two eternally warring factions of 13th-century Florence. In fact, the large, irregular shape of the square isthe result of the destruction of houses and towers belonging to the Ghibelline families, who were expelled from the city in 1258 following a Guelph victory. Considered cursed, the land was not built upon again, thus giving rise to the square that would soon become the heart of Florentine civil and political power. And indeed, the Piazza della Signoria certainly was cursed for Girolamo Savonarola, the preacher who was hanged and burned for heresy on May 23, 1498, after a brief imprisonment in the *alberghetto* ("the little hotel") located halfway up the Torre di Arnolfo of the Palazzo Vecchio ("Old Palace"). A symbolic place in the history of Florence, the tower was opened to visitors in 2012, providing a new viewpoint over the city at a height of 312 feet (95 meters), gained after climbing no fewer than 218 steps. Arnolfo di Cambio's architectural design for the palace represented a model for many large public buildings in 14th-century Tuscany. Originally built as a home for the Priori delle Arti, the building, clad in rusticated stone, became the Palazzo della Signoria in the 15th century, then the residence of the grand ducal family and Cosimo I de' Medici before he transferred to the Palazzo Pitti. The building then became known as the Palazzo Vecchio ("Old Palace"), and it was the grand duke himself who enriched its interior, entrusting its decoration to Giorgio Vasari. Among other works, the artist was also responsible for the frescoes in the grandiose Salone dei Cinquecento ("Hall of the Five Hundred"), built at the end of the 1400s by Savonarola to hold meetings of the Consiglio Maggiore. Inside the Salone is the *Genius of Victory*, Michelangelo's marble masterpiece, and both Michelangelo and Leonardo da Vinci also worked on frescoes for this theatrical space, although these are now lost. And it is Michelangelo who welcomes visitors at the entrance to the Palazzo Vecchio, with a copy of his *David* in the excellent company of *Hercules and Cacus* by Baccio Bandinelli, and a little farther to the right, under the arches of the Loggia dell'Orcagna, Benvenuto Cellini's *Perseus* and the *Rape of the Sabine Women* by Giambologna.

56 *To the right of the Palazzo Vecchio, is the Fontana del Nettuno ("Fountain of Neptune"), by Bartolomeo Ammannati, who was known as "Biancone." A few feet away, a marble plaque marks the place where Dominican friar Girolamo Savonarola was burned as a heretic.*

57 *The Palazzo Vecchio, erected in 1299, is still the heart of the city's civic power. Seat of the Florentine Republic, residence of the Medici, and parliamentary headquarters during Florence's years as Italy's capital, today it houses municipal administrative offices.*

58-59 The courtyard of the Palazzo Vecchio was decorated in 1565, with stuccos and paintings depicting views of the Hapsburg Empire estates, on the occasion of the marriage of Francesco de' Medici and Joanna of Austria.

59 top Savonarola had the Salone dei Cinquecento ("Hall of the Five Hundred") built in 1494—177 feet (54 meters) long and 75 feet (23 meters) wide—to hold the meetings of the Consiglio Maggiore ("Grand Council"). Cosimo I de' Medici later commissioned Vasari to decorate the hall with frescoes.

59 bottom The Loggia dei Lanzi, formerly known as the Loggia dell'Orcagna, owes its name to the German mercenaries who camped there in 1527 (their German name Lanzichenecchi was corrupted to "Lanzi" in Italian). Since the 16th century, great masterpieces of Florentine sculpture have been on show here.

60-61 *Composed of three low-arched spans, the Ponte Vecchio originally had four access towers at its four corners. The only one of these remaining is the Torre dei Mannelli, on the Oltrarno side of the river.*

The View from the Bridge

FLORENCE

Who invented nouvelle cuisine? Few people are likely to know that it was originally served on the Ponte Vecchio ("Old Bridge")—until 1218 the only bridge crossing the River Arno in Florence—by none other than Leonardo da Vinci. A penniless Leonardo, then improvising as a cook, was chased out of the Taverna delle tre Lumache, after offering clients portions that were far too artistic and small for contemporary tastes and stomachs. That was 1473, and the bridge was already the in the form we know today, reconstructed by Taddeo Gaddi, a disciple of Giotto, after a violent flood had destroyed the previous bridge in 1345. The new construction, erected on three arches with deeper and more resilient foundations, had better luck. During the Second World War, it was saved by the German troops, who destroyed only the two medieval buildings at either end of the bridge, preventing access to it, and in 1966 it survived the terrible flood of the Arno that brought Florence to its knees. During Leonardo's time, the famous Vasari Corridor was not yet in place: it was built in just six months by Giorgio Vasari, on the orders of Cosimo de' Medici, to provide an enclosed passageway between the Palazzo Vecchio, the political heart of Florence, and the Palazzo Pitti, the Medici residence. The corridor runs over the top of the Ponte Vecchio's shops, today occupied by goldsmiths, but at the time of the corridor's construction, home to butchers and fruit and vegetable sellers. It was only in 1593 that the unpleasant odors produced by such activities provoked a change, and the small shops gave way to the goldsmiths and their more decorous trade. It was, in fact, in honor of this art that the statue of Benvenuto Cellini, the greatest of the Florentine goldsmiths, was placed on one of the two panoramic terraces at the center of the bridge. For 20 years the iron railings surrounding the monument have had to endure the rather unattractive practice of lovers hanging a padlock on it and then throwing the keys into the Arno: a declaration of love that is as great as the steep fine issued in punishment for the act today.

A Miracle of Marble

PISA

There are probably more columns in the main square of Pisa than there are in rest of Tuscany. A key feature of Pisa's Piazza del Duomo ("Cathedral Square")—renamed Piazza dei Miracoli ("Square of Miracles") in 1910 by Gabriele D'Annunzio—the columns provide an element of continuity between the four sparkling white buildings set in lawns of emerald green. Built in granite from the island of Elba, the columns run in two rows along the central nave of the Cathedral of Santa Maria Assunta. A supreme example of Pisan Romanesque architecture, this "temple as white as snow" was consecrated in 1118 and construction was originally presided over by the architect Buscheto. He was later replaced by Rainaldo, who was responsible for the extension of the nave and the facade, where the columns once again become the main feature in the four tiers of loggia set over blind archways. After completion of the cathedral, construction began on the baptistery in 1152; the largest in Italy, it is dedicated to St. John and was designed by architect Diotisalvi. Its diameter is equal to the width of the cathedral's facade, and there are also references to the cathedral in the baptistery's arches and columns, and the white marble edged with gray. Inside, eight monolithic columns from Elba and Sardinia encircle the octagonal baptismal font, designed by Guido da Como, and the pulpit, a Gothic masterpiece by Nicola Pisano. However, the designer of the square's most famous building, the cathedral bell tower or campanile—universally known as the Leaning Tower of Pisa—is unknown. Circular in shape, like the baptistery, the tower owes most of its international fame to its angle of incline, which, from its foundation in 1173 to the present day, has produced a displacement from the vertical of about 15 feet (4.5 meters)—this has been reduced by 16 inches (40 centimeters) after 12 years of restoration works, concluded in 2001. Since then, visitors have once again been able to climb the 294 steps leading to the belfry, making their way through six tiers of loggias, surrounded by 180 columns. From the top, the views range over the whole square, bordered to the north by the cemetery, a magnificent cloister built in 1277 to house the holy earth brought from Palestine during the Crusades, and also home to the sarcophagi that were once sited around the cathedral. But the most striking aspect of this Camposanto Monumentale ("Monumental Cemetery") is the incredible cycle of 14th-century frescoes covering the interior walls executed by Francesco Traini and Bonamico Buffalmacco among others, including some on the theme of Life and Death. Other frescoes were added subsequently—the *Stories of the Pisan Saints* followed toward the end of the century and, from the mid-1400s, *Stories of the Old Testament* were painted by Benozzo Gozzoli.

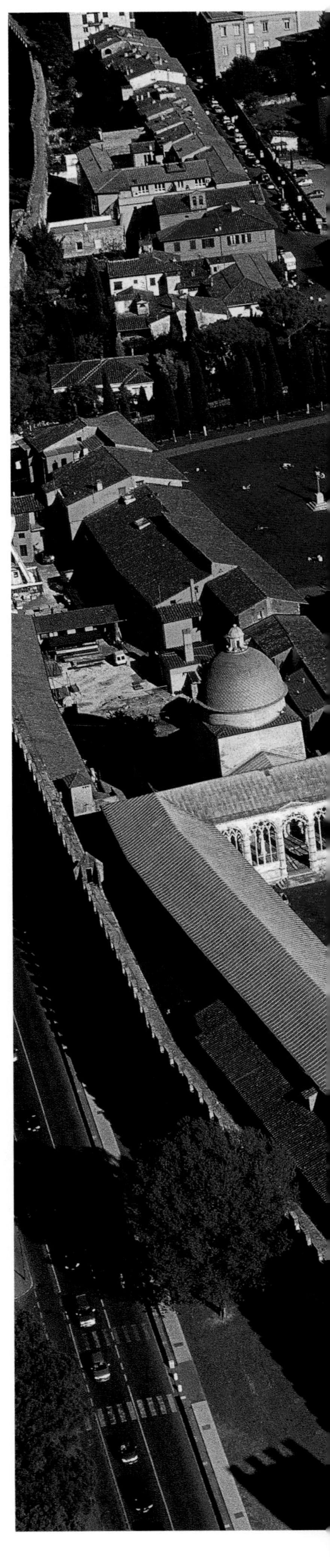

62-63 *The spectacular complex of the Piazza dei Miracoli includes the cathedral, the baptistery, the cemetery, and a certain famous leaning tower, begun in 1173 and later heightened to include three more floors and the belfry.*

GRAND HOTEL

64 *At a height of 180 feet (55 meters) and a circumference of 351 feet (107 meters), the Baptistery of St. John is the largest in Italy. Like the cathedral erected before it, the building is surrounded by arches supported on marble columns with grey bordering.*

65 *The figure of St. John the Evangelist depicted in mosaic in the cathedral apse is the only work by Cimabue whose attribution is based on authoritative documentary sources. It was also the artist's final work.*

66-67 Siena's Piazza del Campo is closed off to the southwest from the Piazza del Mercato by the imposing mass of the Palazzo Pubblico. The palace's bell tower, the Torre del Mangia, owes its name to the first bell ringer, Giovanni di Duccio, known as "Mangiaguadagni."

67 In 1859, the Fonte Gaia, Jacopo della Quercia's 15th-century sculptural masterpiece, was replaced by a copy made of Carrara marble, to protect the fragile Montagnola Senese marble of the original.

The Piazza del Campo, Host to the Explosive Palio

SIENA

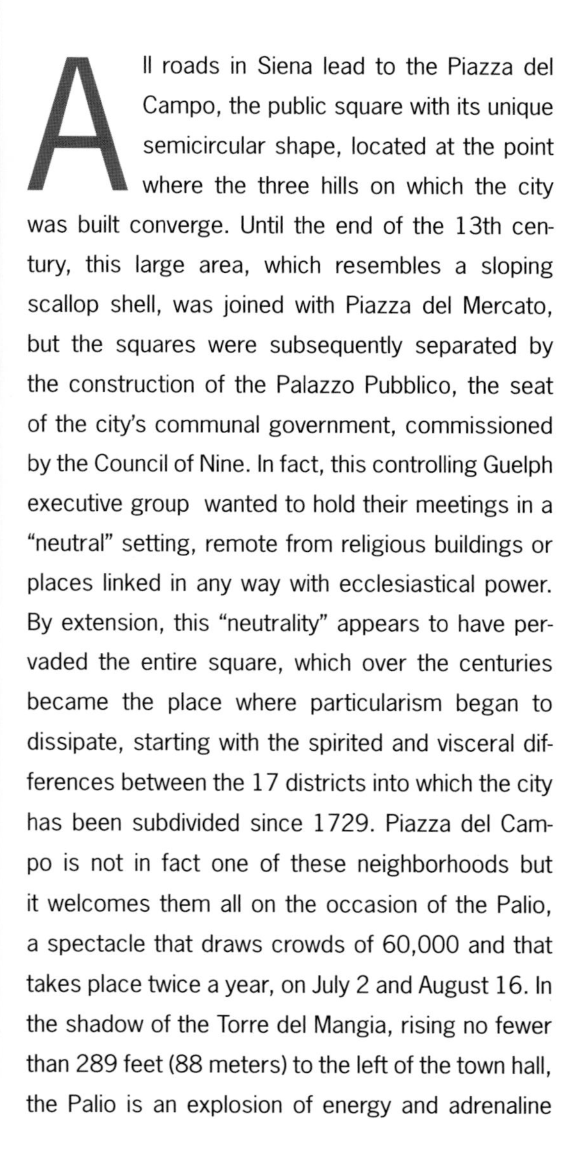

All roads in Siena lead to the Piazza del Campo, the public square with its unique semicircular shape, located at the point where the three hills on which the city was built converge. Until the end of the 13th century, this large area, which resembles a sloping scallop shell, was joined with Piazza del Mercato, but the squares were subsequently separated by the construction of the Palazzo Pubblico, the seat of the city's communal government, commissioned by the Council of Nine. In fact, this controlling Guelph executive group wanted to hold their meetings in a "neutral" setting, remote from religious buildings or places linked in any way with ecclesiastical power. By extension, this "neutrality" appears to have pervaded the entire square, which over the centuries became the place where particularism began to dissipate, starting with the spirited and visceral differences between the 17 districts into which the city has been subdivided since 1729. Piazza del Campo is not in fact one of these neighborhoods but it welcomes them all on the occasion of the Palio, a spectacle that draws crowds of 60,000 and that takes place twice a year, on July 2 and August 16. In the shadow of the Torre del Mangia, rising no fewer than 289 feet (88 meters) to the left of the town hall, the Palio is an explosion of energy and adrenaline that lasts just 75 seconds. That's all it takes for the horses to race three times around the outside edge of the piazza, its 1,112 feet (339 meters) covered in turf for the occasion. It's hard to imagine a more beautiful place for a horse race. Enclosed within the embrace of magnificent medieval palaces, built to specific criteria, which ensured that the greatest architectural harmony was maintained within the designated space, the upper part of the piazza is home to a replica created by Tito Sarrochhi in 1869 of the magnificent Fonte Gaia, a stunning "Quattrocento" fountain built between 1409 and 1419 by Jacopo della Quercia. Since 2011, the original, restored marble panels have been on display in the Fienile section of the Santa Maria della Scala museum complex, flanked by casts from Jacopo della Quercia's original fountain and Tito Sarrocchi's replica.

68 *The celebrated fresco illustrating the taking of Montemassi Castle by Guidoriccio da Fogliano, the captain of the Sienese militia, is in the Palazzo Pubblico's Sala del Mappamondo ("Hall of the World Maps"), in front of Simone Martini's Maestà.*

69 *The fresco Allegory of Good Government by Ambrogio Lorenzetti is in the Sala dei Nove ("Hall of the Nine") at the Palazzo Pubblico; it is part of the cycle commissioned by the republic's administration in 1337.*

The Cathedral: A Choral Masterpiece

SIENA

Siena Cathedral is like a choral work in stone, an extraordinary monument with three naves, dedicated to the *Assumption of the Virgin* Mary, that still seems possessed by the souls of the many artists who contributed to its construction and decoration. Built on the Collina di Santa Maria, the hill that overlooks the entire city, between the late 12th and early 13th centuries, the Duomo, in Romanesque-Gothic style, is one of the most important examples of medieval architecture in Italy. But the cathedral's attractions don't stop at its impressive facade—the lower part of which is the work of sculptor Giovanni Pisano, while the upper part, in ornate Gothic style, is by Giovanni di Cecco—the interior is a veritable feast of art too, starting with the floor. In fact, the cathedral's most astonishing treasure lies beneath the feet of the visitor, framed by the rigorous two-tone black-and-white marbles (the colors of Siena's coat of arms), which can also be seen in the building's facades and in the bell tower. "The most beautiful..., the grandest and most magnificent... ever produced," wrote Giorgio Vasari, about the floor on which some 40 painters and sculptors worked from the 14th century onward. The artists were all Sienese with the exception of Pinturicchio, who was responsible for the "Del Colle della Sapienza" ("Hill of Wisdom") panel, one of the 56 mosaic panels making up this incredible carpet of marble, while 35 of the panels were created by Siena's Domenico Beccafumi. Normally covered to protect them from the cathedral's thousands of visitors, the panels are revealed in all their splendor during the Siena Palio ("Palio di Siena"), when the victorious race winners enter the cathedral to sing the *Te Deum* in thanks. Along the left aisle is another important work by Pinturicchio: the cycle of frescoes depicting events in the life of Pope Pius II, executed by the Perugian artist between 1505 and 1507 for the Libreria Piccolomini, the interior hall built to house the books of Pius II. The cathedral's best-known pictorial masterpiece, however, is no longer in the Duomo: the *Maestà* by Duccio da Buoninsegna, painted between 1308 and 1311 for the main altar, has been exhibited at the Museo dell'Opera—the cathedral museum—since 1878. The museum is housed in the east aisle of the so-called Duomo Nuovo, the cathedral extension undertaken in 1339, but abandoned in 1357 following the terrible plague that struck Siena.

70 *The cathedral's hexagonal cupola is supported by six polystyle columns surmounted by gilded statues of the Sienese saints: Saints Catherine and Bernardino and the city's four patron saints, Ansanus, Savinus, Crescentius, and Victor.*

71 *Two names are principally linked with the construction of the cathedral facade: Giovanni Pisano, who designed the lower part in 1284, and Giovanni di Cecco, who worked on the upper part in 1376, taking inspiration from Orvieto Cathedral.*

72 Scenes from the life of Enea Silvio Piccolomini, who became Pope Pius II in 1458, are portrayed on three walls of the Libreria Piccolomini. Pinturicchio's illustrative biography traces the pope's life from youth to death.

73 The frescoes decorating the three bays toward the back wall of Siena's baptistery were painted by Sienese artist Lorenzo di Pietro, known as "Vecchietta"; begun in 1450, they depict 12 scenes relating to the Apostles' Creed.

CARNIS RESV
RECTIONEM

The "Palace in the Form of a City"

URBINO

A great politician and humanist, Federico da Montefeltro's Studiolo, his small studio on the main floor of the Ducal Palace ("Palazzo Ducale") in Urbino, conveys the stature of the most enlightened figure of the "Quattrocento" (15th century) and the man who lay behind that "palace in the form of a city," the highpoint of Italian Renaissance architecture that would change the face of this town in the Marches forever.

The magnificent marquetry decoration of Federico's meditative retreat depicts the duke's grandiose utopia, illustrating his interests in astronomy, music, the arts, and architecture. Helmets and armor alternate with books, musical instruments, instruments for scientific measurement, landscapes, and portraits that reveal the military leader, ruler, and humanist. A procession of 28 portraits (on wood) of illustrious men marches around the upper part of the studio walls—fitting examinations of each stage of Federico's life. The Dalmatian architect Luciano Laurana designed this "biographical" room and, with Maso di Bartolomeo and Francesco di Giorgio Martini of Siena, made the duke's vision of utopia reality. Laurana is also credited with the Cortile d'Onore ("Court of Honor"), the focal point of the Ducal Palace, considered a masterpiece for its harmonious proportions: it is from here that the palace spreads out in all directions, in unique architectural forms. Of all the facades, the so-called Facciata dei Torricini ("Facade of the Towers"), with its twin towers recognizable from afar, is a masterpiece on a par with the works exhibited in the rooms of the Galleria Nazionale delle Marche, housed in the Ducal Palace, offering a continuous dialogue between the building and its contents. Here in the gallery, where it reached its highest level, the Renaissance art of central Italy can be retraced in works such as the *Flagellation of Christ* and the *Madonna di Senigallia* by Piero della Francesca, the *Communion of the Apostles* by Giusto di Gand ("Justus van Ghent"), the *Miracle of the Profaned Host* by Paolo Uccello, and Raphael's *Portrait of a Young Woman* ("La Muta").

74 The Court of Honor at the Ducal Palace was built by the Dalmatian architect Luciano Laurana between 1466 and 1472. Rhythm and lightness make it one of the showpieces of Urbino's Renaissance architecture.

74-75 Nestled in the hills of the Metauro River Valley, Urbino is one of the great utopias of Quattrocento humanism, an ideal city with the imposing Ducal Palace of the Montefeltros as its symbol.

76 *Federico da Montefeltro's Studiolo, on the main floor of the palace, was created to enhance the figure through painting, with its gallery of portraits of great men and the spectacular trompe l'oeil marquetry work. There are countless symbolic references in the detail of the marquetry. The squirrel intently munching on a nut represents the prudence of Federico who, with the basket filled with fruit, provides for the welfare of his subjects.*

76-77 *Federico da Montefeltro probably commissioned Piero della Francesca to paint the Madonna of Senigallia on the occasion of the marriage of his daughter Giovanna with Giovanni della Rovere, lord of Senigallia.*

The Showcase of Umbria

PERUGIA

You can't blame the young people for choosing to sit, in the evening, on the "*scalette*" of the Cathedral of San Lorenzo, the steps leading up to one side of the Duomo, even if they often are a little noisy. The steps offer a front row seat for the most beautiful view in Perugia as Piazza IV Novembre unfolds before them, a treasure trove of medieval delights, and beyond the square Corso Vannucci, the city's most chic promenade. A short distance from the steps—and from the cathedral's facade, the lower part of which is clad in panels of white and pink marble taken from Arezzo Cathedral—is one of Italy's most famous fountains mounted on a circular base above four steps. The Fontana Maggiore was designed by Fra Bevignate da Cingoli, with decorative sculptures by Nicola and Giovanni Pisano; it made use of water fed into the square from Monte Pacciano. Built between 1275 and 1278, using stone from Assisi, the fountain consists of two concentric polygonal basins decorated with bas-reliefs, featuring themes such as the months of the year and the liberal arts, and is surmounted by a bronze basin adorned with a group of nymphs from which the water spouts. The fountain is at its most striking every summer in early July when it is illuminated in the evenings and a large stage for the Umbria Jazz concerts is set up nearby. Since 1973, the event has been a highlight of Perugia's international calendar, when the square fills with crowds of fans, swaying in time to the music in front of the solid mass of the imposing Palazzo dei Priori, located across the square, opposite the cathedral. Built between 1293 and 1443, the Gothic palace now houses the town hall and the Galleria Nazionale dell'Umbria, the most important collection of Umbrian art from the 13th to 19th centuries. Worth visiting inside the palace are the Sala dei Notari (the notary's room), subdivided by eight transversal arches decorated with allegorical cycles, biblical themes, and fables from Phaedrus and Aesop; the Sala della Mercanzia (the merchandise room); and the Collegio del Cambio (the historic seat of the exchange guild), with frescoes painted in the late 14th century by Perugino.

78 The Palazzo dei Priori, which houses the Galleria Nazionale dell'Umbria and the municipal offices of Perugia, owes its current appearance to the numerous architectural modifications made since the 13th century.

78-79 The heart of Piazza IV Novembre is the 12th-century Fontana Maggiore, built to celebrate the feeding of water through to this part of the city via the new aqueduct from Monte Pacciano.

80 Between 1452 and 1457, the Collegio del Cambio (the guild of money changers), was set up in the Palazzo dei Priori. Perugino was entrusted with the decoration of the Sala delle Udienze (audience hall).

81 God the Father with prophets and sibyls (right, the Eritrean sibyl), in the Allegory of Hope, is part of the decorative program of the lunettes in the Sala delle Udienze (audience hall), with frescoes by Pietro Vannucci, known as "Perugino."

The Gothic Miracle

ORVIETO

The story goes that the birth of one of the greatest architectural masterpieces of the late Middle Ages—Orvieto Cathedral, dedicated to the Assumption of the Virgin—was written in blood. According to tradition it was commissioned by Pope Nicholas IV to contain the Corporal of Bolsena, the blood-soaked linen cloth of the Miracle of Bolsena, when the consecrated host bled into the hands of a priest who had doubts about the real presence of Christ in the Eucharist. Work on the cathedral began in 1290 and this sacred relic is still kept in the Chapel of the Corporal, which was built some years later, like the more famous Chapel of San Brizio, in the space between the load-bearing arches designed by Lorenzo Maitani, the Sienese architect with whom the construction of the cathedral is most closely linked. It was Maitani who gave the new Gothic form to the original Romanesque-style building, which may have been designed by Arnolfo di Cambio. Maitani was responsible, in particular, for the three-gable facade, the lower section of which he personally decorated with bas-relief sculptures. The front of the cathedral, a harmonious amalgam of architecture and decoration, was in fact the result of ongoing work that was not concluded until the late 18th century, with the completion of the magnificent polychrome mosaics on a gold background. Contrasting sharply with the cathedral front, is the black and white rigor of the pillars and walls of the central nave, which, like the external lateral walls, are characterized by alternating bands of travertine and basalt stone. It is color, however, that defines what is considered to be the jewel of the cathedral: the Chapel of San Brizio, dedicated to the patron saint of Orvieto. Initially decorated with frescoes by Fra Angelico assisted by Benozzo Gozzoli, the decoration was subsequently completed with the extraordinary cycle of frescoes by Luca Signorelli dedicated to the Apocalypse and the Last Judgment, a masterpiece of Renaissance painting that was the inspiration for the most famous *Last Judgment* of all times, painted by Michelangelo for the Sistine Chapel.

82 *The sides of the cathedral have remained unchanged from the first architect's original plan; the curved exterior walls of six small chapels are set into them, two of which, less visible, intersect with the transept.*

83 *It took three centuries to build Orvieto Cathedral, a wonderful example of the Romanesque-Gothic style, with a three-gable facade decorated with polychrome mosaics inspired by scenes from the Old and New Testaments.*

DOCTORVM SAPIENS ORDO
MARTIRVM CANDIDATVS EXERCITVS

84-85 BUILT BETWEEN 1408 AND 1444, THE CHAPEL OF THE MADONNA OF SAN BRIZIO OWES ITS NAME TO THE BISHOP WHO BECAME PATRON SAINT OF ORVIETO. IT IS ALSO KNOWN AS THE NEW CHAPEL ("CAPPELLA NUOVA") TO DISTINGUISH IT FROM THE OLDER CHAPEL OF THE CORPORAL.

85 THE COLUMNS IN THE CENTRAL NAVE ARE CHARACTERIZED BY ALTERNATING BANDS OF BASALT AND TRAVERTINE, REFERENCING THE EXTERIOR DECORATIVE MOTIFS. THE INTERIOR OF THE CATHEDRAL DATES BACK TO THE 13TH AND 14TH CENTURIES.

St. Peter's Basilica: Building and Writing History

THE VATICAN CITY, ROME

86-87 *St. Peter's stands on the ruins of the Circus of Nero, where the Apostle Peter was crucified and buried. To honor his memory, in the 4th century Constantine built a basilica with a nave and four aisles over his grave.*

The architects involved in the various stages of St. Peter's construction, for some 120 years, dismantled and rebuilt the basilica consecrated to the first apostle, writing some of the key pages in the history of Italian art between the late Renaissance and early baroque in the process. The seven architects responsible for building of St. Peter's were involved in lengthy battles over almost all aspects, including design, style, ground plans (both Greek and Latin), demolition, and rebuilding. And all this took place under the gaze of no fewer than 20 popes, from Julius II, who in 1506 entrusted Bramante with the construction of a new basilica on the ruins of the one commissioned by Constantine, to Urban VIII, under whose pontificate St. Peter's was finally consecrated. The first architect left behind more rubble than new construction. When Bramante died in 1514, the grandiose temple he designed based upon a Greek cross consisted of only four gigantic columns and as many arches. It was up to Raphael Sanzio to take up the baton, and the artist from Urbino only just had enough time to change the plan to a Latin cross before the task passed to Antonio da Sangallo, who was responsible for raising the level of the basilica floor by 10.5 feet (3.20 meters). Commissioned by Pope Paul III in 1546, Michelangelo went back to Bramante's Greek cross plan from 30 years earlier and designed the cupola, but was only able to construct the drum. And so it was up to Vignola to continue his predecessor's work, while the honor and burden of completing Michelangelo's cupola was left to Giacomo Della Porta and Domenico Fontana, who was commissioned to return to a design based on a Latin cross plan, following the dictates of the Council of Trent, by the addition of two bays. However, this solution was at the expense of the visible impact of the cupola upon the square in front of the basilica, which was greatly diminished. The subsequent design of St. Peter's Square ("Piazzo San Pietro") by Bernini, with its great colonnade, attempts to bring the cathedral closer to the viewer.

88 The dome was decorated between 1603 and 1613 based on 65 sketchings by Cavalier d'Arpino. The glory of God radiates from the eye of the lantern, falling on 96 figures arranged in 6 concentric circles.

89 Designed by Michelangelo, the cupola, or dome, was completed in 1590 by Giacomo della Porta. It has an interior diameter of 139.63 feet (42.56 meters) and a height of 448.06 feet (136.57 meters) to the top of the cross.

Piazza Navona, a Baroque Spectacle

ROME

Where can you find the most beautiful public swimming pool in Rome? For centuries it was in Piazza Navona, the city's baroque square. In fact, in 1652 Pope Innocent X Pamphilj, who owned what was still the most beautiful palace on the square, introduced the tradition of the "Lake of Piazza Navona," offering the city's inhabitants a chance to cool down on the hottest days of the year. During the month of August, the drain in the central fountain was plugged and water was allowed to flood the entire piazza, built on the site of the Stadium of Domitian in the 1st century AD. Ancient Romans would come to the theater to watch Greek athletic games, or *agones*, from which the name Navona derives after various changes of spelling. Even the elongated rectangular shape of the square follows the outline of the Imperial Age arena; it could seat up to 33,000 spectators on the steps of the auditorium, where buildings stand today. Once again, it was Pope Innocent X who was responsible for orchestrating a major transformation in the square. He wanted it to celebrate the prestige of the Pamphilj family. He first commissioned the elegant Palazzo Pamphilj, now home to the Brazilian Embassy since 1929, and then the three fountains that run the length of the piazza: the Fortuna del Nettuno ("Fountain of Neptune") to the north, the Fontana del Moro ("Fountain of the Moor") to the south, and the famous Fontana dei Quattro Fumi ("Fountain of the Four Rivers") by Bernini, in the center. The latter was inaugurated in 1651 and paid for by the proceeds of a very unpopular tax on bread; the largest of the known rivers of the time—the Danube, Nile, Ganges, and Rio de la Plata—are commemorated by giant stone figures, 16 feet (5 meters high), seated on a rocky reef, from which a 50-foot (18-meter) obelisk, previously located at the Circus of Maxentius, rises up. The church of Sant'Agnes in Agone stands opposite this masterpiece of baroque sculpture. It was originally designed by Girolamo Rainaldi and completed in 1652 by Borromini, and has a characteristic concave facade, twin bell towers, and dome. There have been many legends over the centuries about the rivalry between Borromini and Bernini, including the suggestion that the figure representing the Nile is blindfolded in order to avoid seeing the church. In fact, the fountain was constructed first, and the veil over the face of the Nile merely recalls the fact that at that time the sources of the river remained unknown.

90 EACH FLANKED BY TWO DOLPHINS OR OTHER MARINE CREATURES, THE MASCARONS OF THE FONTANO DEL MORO ("FOUNTAIN OF THE MOOR") WERE ORIGINALLY DESIGNED BY GIACOMO DELLA PORTA FOR THE PIAZZA DEL POPOLO FOUNTAIN. IT WAS ONLY IN 1823 THAT VALADIER HAD THEM TRANSFERRED TO THE PIAZZA NAVONA.

90-91 PIAZZA NAVONA, ROME'S MOST BEAUTIFUL BAROQUE SQUARE, FOLLOWS THE DIMENSIONS OF THE ANCIENT DOMITIAN STADIUM, WHICH WAS OVER 886 FEET (270 METERS) LONG AND 180 FEET (55 METERS) WIDE, BUILT BY THE EMPEROR TO HOST THE GREEK ATHLETIC GAMES.

92 The Fortuna del Nettuno ("Fountain of Neptune") at the northern end of the square was known as the "Fountain of the Tinkers," because craftsman producing zinc containers and utensils used to work in this area.

93 Like the Fountain of Neptune, the Fontana del Moro ("Fountain of the Moor") was designed by Giacomo della Porta. The monument owes its name to the sculptural group by Bernini, in which an Ethiopian is shown wrestling with a dolphin.

94-95 and 95 *Nine sculptors worked on the Trevi Fountain, which was designed by Nicola Salvi. Among these were Filippo della Valle, responsible for the statues in the niches at the sides, and Pietro Bracci, who sculpted the Oceanus ("Neptune") group.*

The History and Legend of the Trevi Fountain

ROME

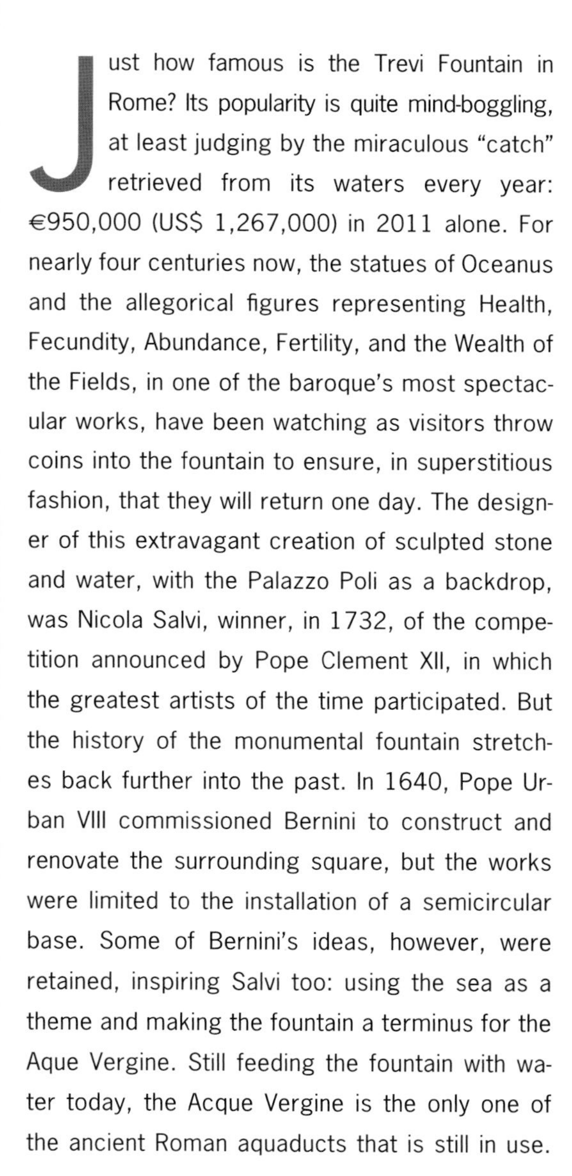

Just how famous is the Trevi Fountain in Rome? Its popularity is quite mind-boggling, at least judging by the miraculous "catch" retrieved from its waters every year: €950,000 (US$ 1,267,000) in 2011 alone. For nearly four centuries now, the statues of Oceanus and the allegorical figures representing Health, Fecundity, Abundance, Fertility, and the Wealth of the Fields, in one of the baroque's most spectacular works, have been watching as visitors throw coins into the fountain to ensure, in superstitious fashion, that they will return one day. The designer of this extravagant creation of sculpted stone and water, with the Palazzo Poli as a backdrop, was Nicola Salvi, winner, in 1732, of the competition announced by Pope Clement XII, in which the greatest artists of the time participated. But the history of the monumental fountain stretches back further into the past. In 1640, Pope Urban VIII commissioned Bernini to construct and renovate the surrounding square, but the works were limited to the installation of a semicircular base. Some of Bernini's ideas, however, were retained, inspiring Salvi too: using the sea as a theme and making the fountain a terminus for the Aque Vergine. Still feeding the fountain with water today, the Acque Vergine is the only one of the ancient Roman aquaducts that is still in use. It was constructed in 19 BC on the orders of the consul Marcus Agrippa, son-in-law of Augustus, to carry water to the new Campus Martius area and its thermal baths. Some 12 miles (20 kilometers) long, the aqueduct ran almost entirely underground. Today, because of groundwater and canal pollution, the water is only used to supply some of the major Roman monuments, including the Fountain of the Four Rivers in Piazza Navona and the Trevi Fountain. It was in the waters of the latter that Federico Fellini filmed Anita Ekberg's legendary bathing scene in *La Dolce Vita*, giving cinema one its iconic images. The fountain brought good luck on this occasion—the film was awarded an Oscar, for Best Costume Design—as it did in 1955 for Jean Negulesco's *Three Coins in the Fountain*, which won two Oscars, for Best Cinematography and Best Original Song.

A Royal Palace Fit for a Bourbon King

CASERTA

A palace that would rival the beauty of Versailles and Schönbrunn; a new residence for the king of Spain's son, who had now become king of Naples: this was the task assigned to Luigi Vanvitelli by Charles III of Spain. The construction of the Palace of Caserta ("Reggia di Caserta") began in 1752 and lasted well over the projected 10 years, costing a total of more than 6 million ducats. It was a colossal construction site, employing 3,000 workers, including 300 foremen, as well as convicts, and Turkish and Christian slaves. Colossal, too, were the dimensions of the palace that the king, recalled to Spain, left for his son King Ferdinand I of the Two Sicilies (also Ferdinand III of Sicily or IV of Naples) and the future husband of Maria Carolina of Austria, who had been born at Schönbrunn, the royal residence that Caserta successfully challenged in the grandeur stakes. The rectangular palace is made up of sections that enclose and overlook 4 inner courtyards. It is intersected by a gallery, which leads all the way from the entrance to the park, creating a telescopic perspective. The palace has over 1,000 rooms arranged over 5 floors and connected by 56 stairways, including the spectacular Honor Grand Staircase. This leads to the upper floors, where we find the Palatine Chapel ("Cappella Palatina"), based on the one at Versailles, and the Royal Apartments, with the immense Throne Room. In Maria Carolina's bathroom is what the Savoys would later describe as "an unknown object in the shape of a guitar," the first bidet known outside France. On the western side of the palace, the court theater (Teatro di Corte) is also remarkable, a miniature copy of the Teatro di San Carlo in Naples. Beyond the stage, a portal opened out onto the Royal Park, the garden designed by Vanvitelli, characterized by its scenic waterway punctuated by fountains, ponds, and waterfalls—all fed by the impressive Caroline Aqueduct, the work of the same architect. Luigi's son Carlo and the English botanist John Graefer created the charming English garden, home to archcitectural features such as the Bath of Venus ("Bagno di Venere"), with simulated ruins of Pompeii, and the Criptoportico, with statues from the excavations of Pompeii.

96 *The Fountain of Venus and Adonis concludes a series of fountains animated by sculptures of mythological themes in the spectacular waterway designed by Luigi Vanvitelli for the Royal Park at the Royal Palace of Caserta.*

97 *Commissioned by Charles III of Spain, the Royal Palace was used primarily as a summer residence. Ferdinand II of the Two Sicilies later chose it as his residence, as did Gioacchino (Joachim) Murat, marshal of France, who fought with Napoleon.*

98-99 *Marble from Atripalda, Dragoni, and Vitulano was used to wonderful and refined decorative effect in the Honor Grand Staircase, a structure 138 feet (42 meters) high and covering 6,458 square feet (600 square meters), making it one of the most spectacular features of the Royal Palace.*

99 *The Throne Room is the largest of the halls in the Royal Apartments. The fresco on the vault, painted by Gennaro Maldarelli in 1844, depicts the placing of the first stone for the Royal Palace of Caserta.*

100-101 *Castel dell'Ovo, the most ancient fortress in Naples, is situated on the tuff island of Megaris (or Megaride), where the small marina of Borgo Marinari can be found, home to Naples' historic sailing clubs.*

101 *The first reports of any sort of fortification on the former island of Megaris are contemporary with the presence of the Basilian monks, but it was the Normans who were responsible for the first castle buildings.*

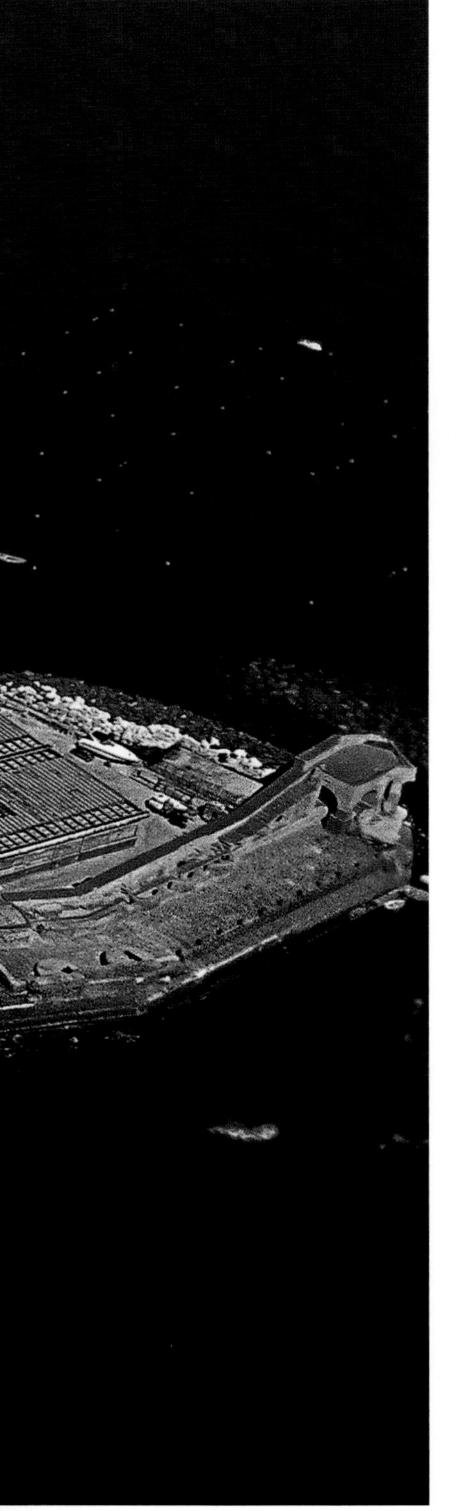

The Egg and the Volcano

NAPLES

Only the world's most superstitious city could name its oldest fortress after the legend that surrounds it. Castel dell'Ovo ("Castle of the Egg"), the fortified island castle, is second only in importance to Vesuvius in the Neopolitan psyche. The story goes that Virgil, the ancient Roman poet from Mantua, believed to be a great sorcerer in medieval times, had hidden in the castle dungeons an egg in a jar of water, which was in turn enclosed in a cage, and that the breaking of this egg would cause the castle to collapse, along with terrible misfortunes for the city of Naples. In 45 BC, Virgil did indeed arrive on Megaris, an island of tuff rock joined to the mainland by a narrow isthmus, and spent 15 years in what previously had been the retreat of the general Lucius Licinius Lucullus, who built a sumptuous villa here surrounded by gardens. The general later passed into history, remembered for his lavish and luxurious banquets (in fact, the term "Lucullian" now refers to this sort of feast). When Virgil died, the villa fell into disrepair, and after serving as a place of exile for Romulus Augustus, the last Western Roman emperor, in 492 it welcomed the Basilian monks, who built the first fortified stronghold as defense against the Saracens. It marked the start of the fortifications that would eventually develop into the castle that visitors see today, a prominent and unmistakable landmark in the Gulf of Naples, opposite the port of Santa Lucia. The Normans, who reached Naples in 1130, constructed the first nucleus of the castle and raised the Normandy Tower ("Torre Normandia"). The Holy Roman Emperor Frederick II added more towers, and the Angevins turned the building into a palace. Following the earthquake of 1370, the latter restored the castle and built a stone reconstruction of the natural arch uniting the two rocky outcrops upon which the fortress rests. It was in the wake of the earthquake that the superstition surrounding the castle resurfaced more powerfully than ever: Queen Joanna I of Naples was obliged to vow to the terrified inhabitants that the castle's egg had been replaced and that Naples was therefore saved. Perhaps that's why, even today, the city still welcomes in the New Year at Castel dell'Ovo with a brilliant display of traditional fireworks that illuminate the fortress and waterfront.

102-103 *The Cathedral of Monreale is Sicily's Norman masterpiece. Waiting to be discovered behind the austere facade are the brilliant mosaics that cover the interior, to the marble plinth.*

103 *A work of art contained within a work of art, the lavatorium, a square structure with pillars containing a fountain ("Chiostrino della Fontana"), reinforces the architectural balance and Arabic style.*

Making a Virtue Out of Diversity

MONREALE

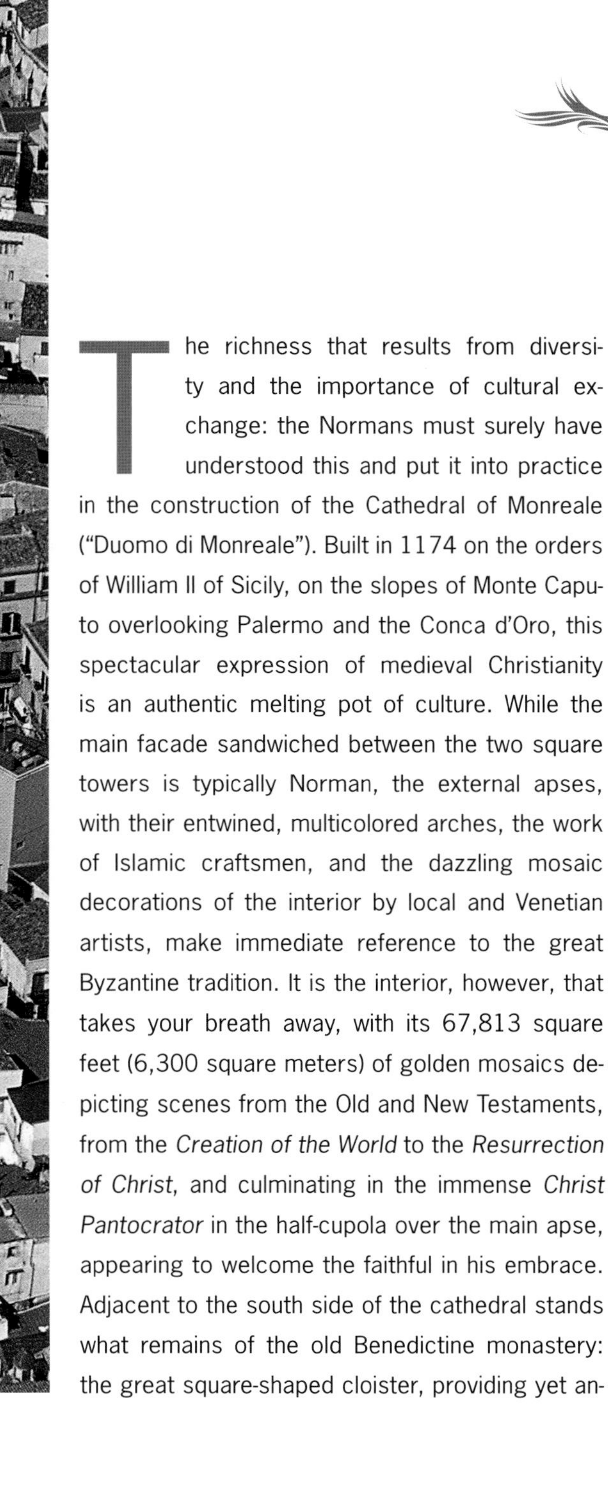

The richness that results from diversity and the importance of cultural exchange: the Normans must surely have understood this and put it into practice in the construction of the Cathedral of Monreale ("Duomo di Monreale"). Built in 1174 on the orders of William II of Sicily, on the slopes of Monte Caputo overlooking Palermo and the Conca d'Oro, this spectacular expression of medieval Christianity is an authentic melting pot of culture. While the main facade sandwiched between the two square towers is typically Norman, the external apses, with their entwined, multicolored arches, the work of Islamic craftsmen, and the dazzling mosaic decorations of the interior by local and Venetian artists, make immediate reference to the great Byzantine tradition. It is the interior, however, that takes your breath away, with its 67,813 square feet (6,300 square meters) of golden mosaics depicting scenes from the Old and New Testaments, from the *Creation of the World* to the *Resurrection of Christ*, and culminating in the immense *Christ Pantocrator* in the half-cupola over the main apse, appearing to welcome the faithful in his embrace. Adjacent to the south side of the cathedral stands what remains of the old Benedictine monastery: the great square-shaped cloister, providing yet another demonstration of the cosmopolitan nature of Norman art, with its 208 richly decorated columns culminating in variously sculpted capitals, supporting arches that clearly derive from the Arabic tradition. The new Museo Diocesano di Monreale ("Diocesan Museum") offers views of the cloister and its garden, but also of its mosaics, the exterior of the apse, and over the Gulf of Palermo. Inaugurated in 2011, the museum was 20 years in the making, a long time considering that in the 12th century the entire cathedral was built in just over half of that. However, the wait has been rewarded with three exhibition floors in the building of the historic Seminario Maggiore part of the Palazzo Arcivescovile ("Archbishop's Palace"), housing the treasure of Sicily's largest diocese, with works and artifacts of sacred art dating from 1200 to 1800.

104 *The cathedral faces east, in accordance with Byzantine tradition. The nave and two aisles have two rows of nine granite columns. The nave culminates in the celebrated mosaic work Christ Pantocrator.*

104-105 *The cathedral's minor apses are decorated with golden mosaic portraits, depicting the holy men who followed Christ's example. The apse to the right is dominated by the figure of St. Peter.*

In Sicily's Garden of Stone

Make a virtue of necessity: that's what the towns and villages in the province of Ragusa had to do, after being razed to the ground by the terrible earthquake that destroyed nearly all of southeastern Sicily on January 6, 1693. Trying to make the best of the disaster that killed over half the population in Ragusa alone, the towns rose again, this time in a single architectural style, the baroque, and have now rightfully been inscribed on UNESCO's World Heritage List alongside other sites that were rebuilt in the Valle di Noto. The area positively overflows with a wealth of architectural heritage; everywhere you look churches, convents, and aristocratic palaces impress with their extravagant decoration. Beneath the balconies are highly ornate corbels that seem to have emerged from the hands of the architect; grotesque masks, putti, female figures, turbaned servants, bunches of flowers, and musical instruments are illustrations in stone of the irrepressible creative imagination of the late baroque period. An outstanding example is Palazzo Beneventano in Scicli, with its human caricatures and fantastical animals decorating the facade. It is an 18th-century masterpiece, like the churches and palaces overlooking Via Mormino Penna, Scicli's most atmospheric street, with buildings in the baroque, neoclassical, and Liberty styles. The city of Ragusa is extremely beautiful; it is divided into two distinct parts: Ragusa Inferiore (Ibla), the heart of the city, full of churches and aristocratic palaces, laid out according to the old medieval plan, and Ragusa Superiore, the Upper Town that grew up on the high plateau after the 1693 earthquake. The focal point of Ibla, and the work of Rosario Gagliardi, the Sicilian baroque's most important architect, the Cathedral of San Giorgio is situated at a slight angle overlooking the square below, which it dominates with its imposing facade. Also by Gagliardi is a second Cathedral of San Giorgio, this time in Modica. Considered the absolute masterpiece of late baroque architecture, it lies between the upper and lower parts of the city, at the top of a dizzying flight of 250 steps.

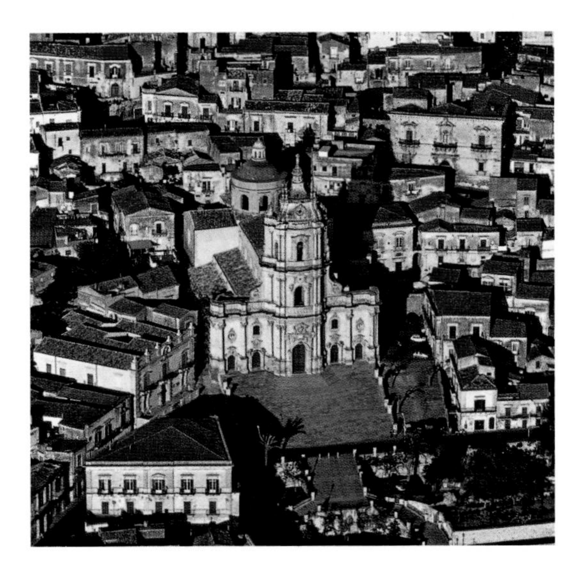

106 *The Cathedral of San Giorgio, built between the upper and lower parts of Modica, is attributed to Rosario Gagliardi, the architect who left his mark, more than any other, in the late baroque architecture of the provinces of Ragusa and Syracuse.*

107 *The Two Moors' heads are the irreverent sculpted decorations on a cornerstone that, like a clasp, join the two identical facades of Palazzo Beneventano in Ragusa, one of the baroque masterpieces of Scicli.*

The Grand Tour in Italian Art

In order to understand the true grandeur of Italy's artistic heritage and to grasp the sheer enormity of the legacy left by artists working on the peninsula from the Middle Ages to today, we need to forget the contemporary world, with its Internet, televisions, telephones, trains, and highways. The great Italian artists may not have had any means of fast communication, but they had huge creative energy and left behind magnificent frescoes, paintings, and sculptures in Rome, Venice, Umbria, and Florence, in both religious and civic locations, highlighting their importance and ensuring their immortality.

Retracing the path of the history of Italian art involves accompanying the Italian masters of figurative art on their journeys, both real and artistic, and observing the development of their own unique artistic language. To retrace the path of the history of Italian art we must accompany the Italian masters of figurative art on their journeys, both real and artistic, and observe the development of their unique artistic language.

Selecting the best chapters in the rich story of Italian art as told through its churches, museums, and city squares is virtually an impossible task. This selection therefore concentrates on key turning points, on the works and artists who have contributed, in minor or major ways, to the story of Italy's artistic identity. It is a collection, indeed a whole gallery of masterpieces, all of which are superb in their own way.

As with any developmental process, that of art comes from a form of detachment or departure, and in this context it was a departure from the pictorial language of the Byzantine tradition. It was the artist Cimabue who was responsible for this revolutionary rift or transformation; in his Santa Trinita Maestà *("The Madonna in Majesty"), he takes the first steps in the search to conquer space, moving from the tradition of two-dimensional depictions to a new three-dimensionality, achieved through the concave structure of the throne on which the madonna sits. His work does not feature traditional Byzantine rigidity, but instead has an unprecedented intensity of expression. Giotto, a pupil of Cimabue, then achieved true independence from the Oriental tradition with his transformative entry into the history of Italian art. In his frescoes, the Tuscan painter gives substance to the figures, transferring Gothic sculpture into painting and giving the illusion of depth and volume to the flat surface. In the cycle of the* Life of Saint Francis *in the Upper Basilica of San Francesco of Assisi, the figures are vividly real, making the viewers feel as if they are actual participants in the narration of events. The painted word of the artist found a new voice in Padua in the splendid frescoes in the Scrovegni ("Arena") Chapel, in which Giotto makes wonderful use of chiaroscuro to bring both realism and volume to his figures, which are astonishing both for their physical and psychological characterization. This same introspection becomes evident later in the discipline of sculpture too, with Donatello's* David. *The humanity in the face of the young biblical hero is wholly innovative and bears witness to a rebirth of art that would spread from Florence throughout the country, culminating in the Italian Renaissance of the 16th century with Michelangelo Buonarroti, who sculpted another great Florentine* David. *Vasari wrote that the beauty of Michelangelo's* David *"carried off the palm from all other statues, modern or ancient."*

The banks of the River Arno were a hotbed of artistic endeavor during this period, with the creation of masterpieces such as Botticelli's Allegory of Spring ("Primavera") *and Leonardo's* Annunciation, *which are among the best loved works in the Uffizi Gallery, united by their portrayal of two of the most beautiful flowering meadows in Italian art. Another key work of the 15th century is the sacred painting by Mantegna of the* Lamentation over the Dead Christ. *Housed at the Pinacoteca di Brera, it represents another turning point in Italian art, with its dramatic qualities and unprecedented foreshortening of the recumbent figure. Mantegna's work in Milan is in excellent company. In the same gallery is another Renaissance icon, Raphael's* Marriage of the Virgin, *and in the refectory of Santa Maria delle Grazie hangs one of the world's most famous paintings, Leonardo da Vinci's* Last Supper. *It was Ludovico the Moor, a great patron of the arts, who commissioned the latter. Leonardo was sent to his court by Lorenzo the Magnificent, one of the greatest promoters of art of his time and the man to whom the history of Italian art owes the largest number of masterpieces, not least those of Michelangelo. The years he spent studying at the court of the Medicis were crucial to Buonarroti's artistic development. Empowered by his knowledge of 15th-century Florentine art, he arrived in Rome already capable of achieving the sublime, not only in sculpture, with his magnificent* Pietà *at the Vatican, but also in painting, as revealed by his frescoes for the Sistine Chapel. This period is now referred to as the late Renaissance, which saw Rome become the new capital of the arts, with artists such as Raphael and Bramante working at the same time as Michelangelo. It was during this time that the most accomplished artists also converged in Venice, among them Giorgione and Titian, who were major innovators. With his* Tempest, *Giorgione signed the manifesto of tonal painting, the use of color to construct space; and with his* Sacred and Profane Love, *Titian left to the history of Italian art one of its most controversial and mysterious paintings. Another famous Venetian painting was equally controversial:* The Feast in the House of Levi, *by Veronese, which landed him before the court of the Inquisition. The Council of Trent, a major reform council, had only recently come to an end, and along with it the spirit of the Renaissance. The renewal of painting at the end of the 16th century saw the emergence of the key figure of Caravaggio, the master of realism. His* Basket of Fruit *paved the way for a new genre of painting, still life, and would become the jewel in the collection of Cardinal Federico Borromeo.*

This journey through the wonders of Italian art concludes at the Galleria Borghese, home of another great collector, Scipione Borghese, where the vitality of two sculptures, Bernini's Apollo and Daphne *and Canova's* Venus Victrix, *demonstrates just how far, in terms of both artistic endeavor and time, art had traveled from the Byzantine when it all began.*

Cimabue's *Maestà di Santa Trinita*

Revolutionary and avant-garde, Cimabue—the pseudonym for the artist Cenni di Pepo—was the first painter who, although still tied to the past, understood the importance of looking to the future. These themes are clearly evident in the *Santa Trinita Maestà* ("The Madonna in Majesty"), a work commissioned by the monks of Vallombrosa for the high altar in the Florentine church of the same name. The work was later transferred to the monastery's infirmary and then, for more than a century, exhibited in the room at the Uffizi Gallery dedicated to the 13th century and Giotto. The large wooden altarpiece references traditional Byzantine iconography, but also introduces innovative elements heralding the great transformations in art that were to come with the 14th century. Cimabue depicts the enthroned madonna with child, flanked by four angels on each side. The representation is viewed from the front, but the throne has a concave structure, suggesting a depth that is also expressed by the angels, who are slightly offset from one another, and by the prophets, depicted in half-bust portraits in the three niches beneath the throne. Jeremiah and Isaiah, to the sides, and Abraham and David at the center, communicate, through their gazes, their positions in space to the observer. The background is still flat and golden as in Byzantine tradition, but with the new naturalistic perspective of the *Santa Trinita Maestà*, Cimabue paves the way for Giotto and his brilliant "conquest of space." But like all great revolutionaries, Cimabue too was misunderstood, to the extent that he inspired a rather barbed triplet from Dante: "Once Cimabue thought to hold the field / as painter; Giotto now is all the rage, / dimming the luster of the other's fame" (*Purgatory*, Canto 11). These verses immediately come to mind in Room 2 of the Uffizi, where a comparison of these Maestà, or Majesty, paintings is inevitable: with the *Santa Trinita* by Cimabue and the one painted by Giotto for the church at Ognissanti sitting under the same beamed ceiling, as well as the *Rucellai Madonna* by Duccio di Buoninsegna, a work so noticeably influenced by Cimabue's painting that it was attributed to him up until the end of the 19th century.

110 AND 111 *CIMABUE'S REPRESENTATION OF THE MADONNA ENTHRONED WITH CHILD REFERENCES BYZANTINE ICONOGRAPHY. BELOW THE THRONE, ON EITHER SIDE, ARE THE PROPHETS JEREMIAH AND ISAIAH, AND IN THE CENTER, BETWEEN THEM, ABRAHAM AND DAVID.*

The Basilica of St. Francis of Assisi
Giotto's Frescoes

The history of the Basilica of St. Francis of Assisi and its frescoes changed on September 26, 1997. On that day, an earthquake measuring 9 on the Mercalli and up to 6.1 on the Richter scale caused the death of 4 people and the collapse of 3,014 square feet (280 square meters) of murals in the Upper Basilica. Among these, 861 square feet (80 square meters) of a painting of St. Jerome attributed to the young Giotto exploded into 80,000 fragments. These were reassembled, and after 65 percent of the work was restored, it was returned to its original place. The incredible reconstruction site was known as the "worksite of Utopia," but it became very real following its restoration of 51,700 square feet (4800 square meters) of frescoes by Cimabue, Jacopo Torriti, Pietro Cavallini, and, of course, Giotto, which were marked by 19 miles (30 kilometers) of cracks. The 28 restored panels dedicated to the life of St. Francis, painted by Giotto in the last decade of the 13th century, were returned to their former glory. The artist painted the works for the Lower Basilica, inspired by the *Legenda Maior*, the biography of St. Francis by St. Bonaventure. Framed by columns, the vivid scenes appear to reach out to greet the observer, thereby establishing a relationship between the painted space and the real space of the soaring

112 AND 113 *DESIGNED BY BROTHER ELIAS OF CORTONA, WORK BEGAN ON THE UPPER BASILICA OF ST. FRANCIS OF ASSISI (OPPOSITE, NAVE WITH 4 BAYS), ALONG WITH THE LOWER BASILICA, THE DAY AFTER THE SAINT WAS CANONIZED IN 1228.*

basilica, constructed in the French Gothic style and housing the largest cycle of frescoes from the 13th and 14th centuries, known as the Italian Duecento and Trecento. The *Life of St. Francis* has its own important date in history. Many view this impressive visual narrative as heralding the arrival of modernity and the passage of art from " Greek" to "Latin." It marked the liberation from the flat, two-dimensional Byzantine style of medieval painting to make way for realistic three-dimensional representations of space that gave images physical concreteness. Further witnesses to this revolution can be found in the frescoes painted by Giotto with his collaborators, from 1307, for the Lower Basilica at Assisi. It had the same plan as the Upper Basilica but is more like a crypt, a place inviting contemplation and prayer before the mortal remains of the saint, laid to rest beneath the basilica itself.

114 Sermon to the Birds *is the 15th of 28 scenes dedicated to the* Life of St. Francis, *on which work began in 1296, frescoed by Giotto in the lower part of the nave of the Upper Basilica.*

115 *The use of foreshortened buildings and structures as backdrops for characters is particularly evident in* The Expulsion of the Devils from Arezzo, *the 10th story in the cycle dedicated to St. Francis.*

The Scrovegni Chapel Giotto's Frescoes

Giotto's work must have exceeded even the most optimistic expectations of the man who commissioned them. Enrico Scrovegni was a wealthy banker from Padua with a great desire for redemption both for himself but, more importantly, for his father Reginaldo, who was known to be a usurer (lending money at very high rates of interest). Today, the construction of a chapel attached to the family palace would be viewed as a marketing exercise, and it was so successful that on March 25, 1303, the day of the dedication to honor the Feast of the Annunciation, everyone was dumbstruck, including Scrovegni. For the first time, a ray of light traversed the large space of the single nave and struck a point on the fresco of the *Last Judgment*, exactly between the hand of the figure of Enrico and the hand of the Virgin as she receives the gift of the chapel from the banker. Two years earlier the visionary Scrovegni had called Giovanni Pisano to Padua to commission the three altar statues representing the Madonna and Child positioned between two deacons. He entrusted to Giotto the entire task of painting what was originally conceived as a funerary chapel for the Scrovegni family. Giotto, who had already been commissioned by Pope Boniface VIII to paint frescoes in the Upper Basilica at Assisi and in St. John Lateran, took 850 days to complete his masterpiece in Padua, which recounts the story of Christ and the Virgin over a surface of almost 3,280 square feet (1,000 square meters). It begins with the story of St. Joachim and St. Anne, father and mother of Mary, and ends with the *Last Judgment*, which fills the space of the entire counter-facade of the chapel. The harmony between the architecture and the paintings is so striking that some scholars believe that Giotto may also have been responsible for the chapel's design. On its walls, the Tuscan painter transforms the religious story into a contemporary human drama, filling the frescoes with figures dressed in 14th-century costume and examples of Gothic architecture. As he did in part in Assisi, Giotto puts into practice his research into perspective, creating illusions of depth through color alone. The key work carried out by the Central Institute of Restoration of Italy, completed only in 2002, managed to highlight his powerful use of chiaroscuro.

116 *The harmony between painting and architecture is so exceptional that Giotto is believed to have also been the architect for the Arena Chapel in Padua, in addition to having frescoed the entire single-nave interior.*

118-119 *In his* Lamentation over the Dead Christ, *Giotto moves forward from the Gothic-Byzantine tradition by introducing veiled figures in the background, adding a new realism to the representation of the scene.*

119 *The spears and torches moving against the blue background suggest a sense of depth in* Kiss of Judas, *while the alternating warm and cooler colors add volume to the figures.*

Donatello's *David*

Donatello's *David* has a slightly impertinent expression; it was the first nude statue of the Renaissance and the first work since ancient Roman times to be portrayed in the round, without either background or veils (if we exclude the bronze crucifix created by the same artist for the Basilica of St. Anthony in Padua). The recently restored sculpture that can be admired today at the Bargello Museum ("Museo Nazionale del Bargello") in Florence is of a young, almost ephebic David, whose eyes reveal his pride—he seems both amazed and pleased at having vanquished the giant Goliath, a sort of declaration of the supremacy of cunning and intellect over strength. The future king of Israel, supporting his right leg with his sword while his left leg stamps on the head of his vanquished enemy, is wearing knee-high ancient-world sandals and an unusual hat with a broad brim at the front, similar to the petasus worn by Hermes—elements that have led many historians to interpret the work as a depiction of this pagan god who defeated Argos. A number of mysteries surround Donatello's *David*, not just about its meaning, but also who commissioned it and when it was created. Among the most credible hypotheses is one claiming that Cosimo "the Elder" de' Medici commissioned the work for the Casa Vecchia ("Old House") on Via Larga around 1435. From here, the statue would follow its owner to the Palazzo Medici (today, the "Palazzo Medici Riccardi"), where its positioning, at the center of the courtyard, was first documented in a social chronicle from 1469, which was a description of the marriage of Lorenzo the Magnificent and Clarice Orsini. Here, the 5 foot 2 inches tall (158 centimeter) bronze was placed on top of a column created by Desiderio da Settignano, a pupil of Donatello himself. With the expulsion of the Medici from Florence in 1495, *David*'s long journey began—with stops at the Palazzo Vecchio, Palazzo Pitti, and the Uffizi—which finally in 1865 brought it to the newly created Museo Nazionale del Bargello, in the company of the greatest masterpieces of Florentine statuary, including another *David* by Donatello; this one was sculpted in marble by the artist in 1408 for cathedral of Santa Maria del Fiore.

120 AND 121 *THE BRONZE* DAVID, *62 INCHES (158 CENTIMETERS) TALL, DATES FROM THE HEIGHT OF DONATELLO'S MATURITY AS AN ARTIST. THE WORK IS FIRST MENTIONED IN 1469, IN A RECORD REFERRING TO THE MARRIAGE OF LORENZO THE MAGNIFICENT AND CLARICE ORSINI.*

Sandro Botticelli's *Allegory of Spring*

When studying Botticelli's *Primavera* (in full, "*The Allegory of Spring*"), a Renaissance masterpiece housed at the Uffizi Gallery, viewers can observe grace, elegance, and an entire world—that of the 15th-century Florence ruled by Lorenzo de' Medici, also known as Lorenzo Il Magnifico ("the Magnificent"). Like other works by Botticelli with an allegorical and mythological character, this painting is a vital celebration of the happiest of all periods in Florence's history, and it reflects the cultural climate of the time. The painting was probably commissioned by a Medici cousin, Lorenzo di Pierfrancesco, but it was at Il Magnifico's house that Giorgio Vasari—the man credited with naming the work—first saw it. From that moment on, there has been much debate about the significance of the painting, but all interpretations agree on one theme being the exaltation of beauty as a means of transcending matter—and this was a key aspect of Neoplatonism, the philosophical and aesthetic movement that revolved around the Medici court, and which had Marsilio Ficino and Pico della Mirandola as exponents. But who are the nine figures who appear to be almost dancing in the air above a lawn, against the backdrop of a grove of orange trees? The most commonly accepted interpretations of who these figures are as follows, from right to left. A blue-colored figure, perhaps the personification of the Spring Wind, seizes the nymph Chloris who, as detailed in Ovid's *Fasti,* was transformed into Flora: here the third figure wearing a floral-patterned garment. She is scattering flowers over a blossoming carpet, in which Botticelli included no fewer than 190 different botanical species, in all probability inspired by the Flemish Millefleurs tapestries. Positioned slightly farther back, at the center of the painting, is an elegant woman, over whose head a blindfolded cherub, perhaps Cupid, hovers, intent on shooting an arrow. In the Neoplatonic interpretation, this central maiden—often identified as Venus—is the manifestation of Humanitas, the intermediary between man and God, who separates material delights on the right, from spiritual ones on the left, as embodied by the three Graces dancing and by Mercury. This final figure, the god of war, completes Botticelli's allegory by chasing away the clouds with his caduceus (or wand), thus ensuring an eternal spring.

123 and 124-125 *The nymph Chloris, transformed into Flora by Zephyr, is one of the 9 characters animating Sandro Botticelli's Primavera (tempera on panel; 80 x 124 inches/203 x 314 centimeters) painted between 1477 and 1478.*

Leonardo da Vinci's *Annunciation*

126-127 *Leonardo da Vinci painted* The Annunciation *(oil and tempera on panel; 39 x 85 inches/98 x 217 centimeters) for the refectory of the Olivetan monastery of San Bartolomeo outside Florence while in his early twenties (1472–75).*

In the 1980s, Andy Warhol needed just a few details to create his homage to Leonardo da Vinci's *Annunciation*. Famous for his "Marilyns" and his Campbell's soup cans, Warhol was moved by the picture and its poetic simplicity, painted by a youthful Leonardo around 1475. By reproducing only the hands of the Archangel Gabriel and the Virgin Mary, but depicting them making the same gestures as in the painting by the most eclectic of the Renaissance masters, Warhol paid tribute to the painting's expressive majesty in his own way. In the Uffizi's collection since 1867 and long attributed to Ghirlandaio, the work reveals Leonardo the experimenter and innovator, an artist who, rather than choosing to revel in intellectualism, aims toward truth and the presentation of reality as we all see it. The waterscape and mountainous landscape in the background of the picture demonstrate this, making use of perspective, with the more distant details appearing somewhat blurred, just they are perceived with the naked eye. The position of the landscape at the center of the picture confirms a recent hypothesis, suggesting that the painting was conceived not for viewing directly from the front, but rather from an angle. Viewed from the lower right-hand corner, many of the alleged errors in perspective attributed to Leonardo over the years, disappear: the Madonna becomes more central, and her arm, initially seen as too long, assumes more natural proportions; the facade of the palace behind her lengthens, and the lectern, apparently too far forward from Mary, comes closer, so that the position of the arm is more natural. Especially interesting is the sarcophagus on which the lectern is standing. It is a reproduction, in fact, of the one created by Verrocchio for the tomb of Giovanni and Piero de' Medici in the Old Sacristy in the Basilica of San Lorenzo, in Florence. A tribute by Leonardo to his master, in whose workshop he was raised and under whose protection he still was at the time of painting the *Annunciation*.

Andrea Mantegna's *Lamentation of Christ*

Andrea Mantegna's *Lamentation of Christ* seizes the attention immediately. The converging lines of the composition, depicting the body ready for burial, with wounds in the hands and feet, pulls the viewer into the heart of the drama. The painting conveys the emotional shock of the moment, reflected in the statue-like faces of the grieving: the Madonna drying her tears, Saint John with his hands clasped in prayer, and in the background, an indistinct figure, probably Mary Magdalene. Lying on the Stone of Anointing, Jesus is viewed from the front, limp on the stone slab, his whole body visible. Mantegna did not respect the rules of perspective entirely, instead distorting them slightly, so that the painting seems to follow you around the room. As you approach the picture, the feeling is one of realism, of truly looking upon a person who has died, like the three grieving figures, almost sacrificed, at the left of the canvas. Everything in this image speaks of the tragedy of the death of Christ, beginning with the realistic depiction of the cruel wounds in the hands and feet. Part of the collection at the Pinacoteca di Brera, the Christ portrayed by Mantegna is of flesh and blood, shown in his full humanity, not idealized, as can be seen from the genitals, clearly visible beneath the shroud, which is draped as in classical sculpture. This powerful representation, with its incredible expressive force, was probably kept by the great painter of the *Camera degli Sposi* ("The Bridal Chamber") until the end of his days. Discovered in Mategna's studio after his death, it seems, in fact, that this "foreshortened Christ" was used by the artist for his private devotion. First sold by his son to Cardinal Sigismondo Gonzaga, the painting later passed to Charles I of England, and then to Cardinal Mazarin, who served as first minister of France. After disappearing for more than a century, in 1824 it finally entered the Brera Gallery at the request of Giuseppe Bossi, then secretary of the academy, and thanks to the mediation of one of the great artists of the time, Antonio Canova.

128-129 *Discovered in the artist's workshop after his death in 1506, the expressive power of Mantegna's Lamentation of Christ (tempera on canvas; 27 x 32 inches/68 x 81 centimeters) marks it out as an Italian Renaissance masterpiece.*

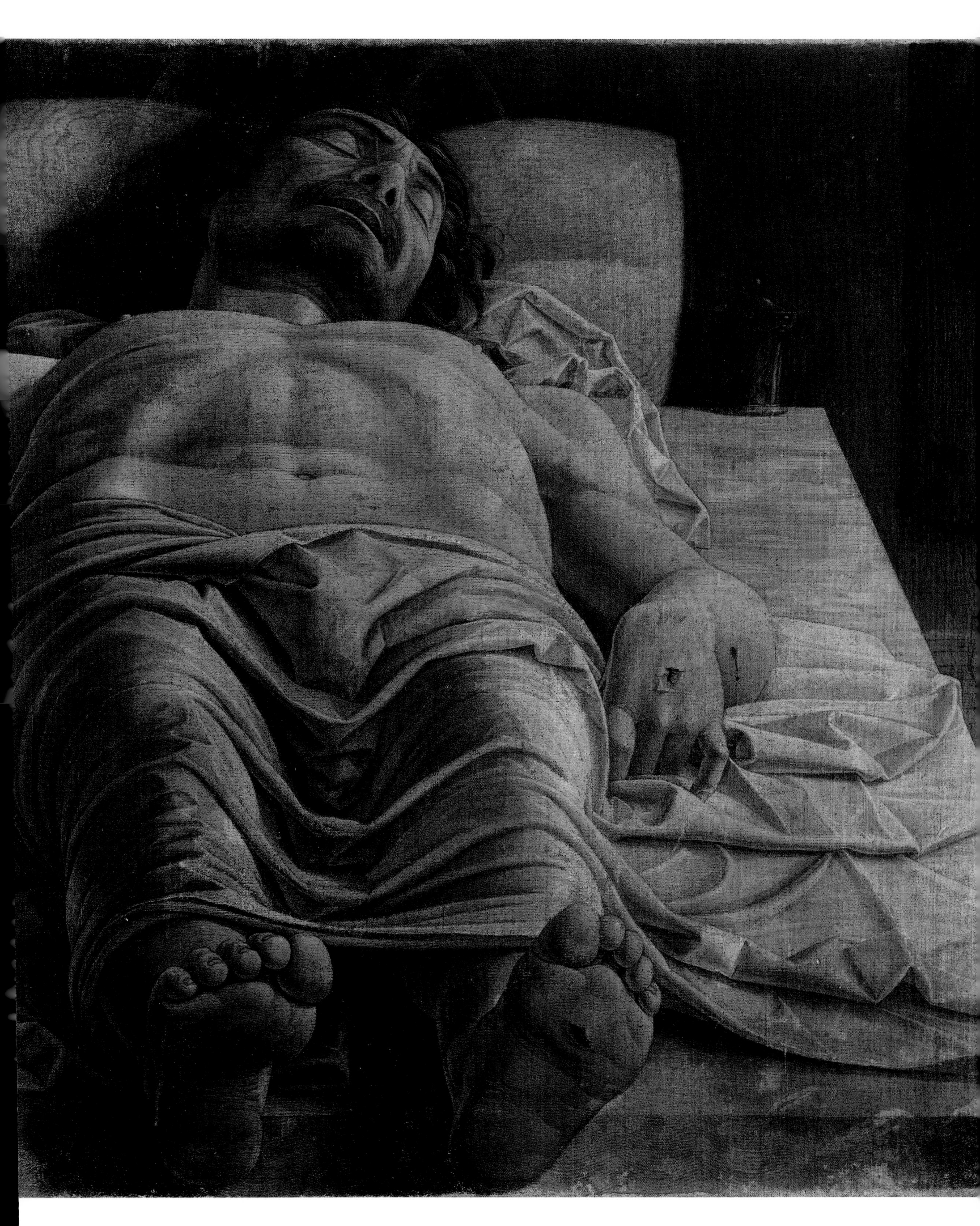

Leonardo da Vinci's *Last Supper*

130-131 Painted in the refectory of the Dominican convent of Santa Maria delle Grazie in Milan, and commissioned by Ludovico Il Moro, Leonardo's Last Supper represents a thorough study of the human soul.

The *Last Supper?* To understand how Leonardo's masterpiece looked when first painted, we need to take a short tour of Europe, to Magdalen College in Oxford, England, where the copy by Leonardo's assistant, Giampietrino, is held, or to Écouen, north of Paris, where the copy attributed to Marco d'Oggiono can be seen in the Museum of the Renaissance. The painting that visitors see today on the rear wall of the Santa Maria delle Grazie convent refectory in Milan is very different from the one Ludovico il Moro saw in 1497, the year Leonardo completed the work commissioned by the duke of Milan. An incorrect decision lies behind the deterioration in the work that has since taken place: Leonardo painted onto the wall using the medium of *tempera grassa,* as though painting on a panel, rather than use the fresco technique. The tempera technique with which the Renaissance genius was experimenting, proved vulnerable to humidity and to the passage of time. And so, despite the restoration work carried out between 1979 and 1999, much of the original image has now been lost. If the blue tones have been restored to their previous brilliance, the greens have practically disappeared. The Apostles' feet, however, have returned, whereas those of Christ are lost forever, with the opening of a passageway that connected the refectory to the kitchens. What still enchants is Leonardo's portrayal of the events of the *Last Supper*, depicting the human drama of the betrayal by probing into the psychology of the Apostles, who are positioned in the composition in four groups of three, arranged symmetrically around Christ. The revelation of Jesus is shown by Leonardo as a wave emerging from the center and rippling out toward the ends of the table in varying degrees of intensity. Gestures, facial expressions, and the position of hands embody the theory of "movements of the soul" on which all of Leonardo's painting was based: details allowing the viewer to understand the emotional reaction of each of the Apostles. A world of feelings that British director Peter Greenaway revisited in 2008 at the Palazzo Reale ("Royal Palace") in Milan, with a multimedia event of great poetry, when colors and details that had seemed lost forever were restored to the Renaissance masterpiece.

RAPHAEL·VRBINAS
M
DIIII

Raphael Sanzio's *Marriage of the Virgin*

On August 15, 1809, on the occasion of Napoleon's birthday, the Pinacoteca di Brera opened to the public for the first time. In March of 2009, this great Milanese museum celebrated its bicentenary by showcasing the restoration of Raphael's *The Marriage of the Virgin*, the painting that—along with Mantegna's *Lamentation over the Dead Christ* and Piero della Francesca's *Brera Madonna* (also called the *Montefeltro Altarpiece*)—best represents the Brera collection. Stolen from the Church of San Francesco at Città di Castello in Perugia by General Lechi, at the time in the service of Napoleon, Raphael's work reached Milan in 1805, endowing prestige to the nascent collection and soon becoming its cornerstone. Dated 1504, Raphael painted the work for the Albizzini chapel in the Church of San Francesco when he was barely 20 years old, but already mature and on the verge of moving to Florence, and it represents a sort of declaration of independence by the artist from Urbino. While the *Marriage* can be seen as a pupil's tribute to his master, Perugino, it clearly demonstrates that the pupil has surpassed the master. Raphael's work contains obvious references to Perugino's altarpiece on the same subject painted for the Chapel of the Holy Ring in the Duomo at Perugia, now conserved in Caen, France. The iconography is the same, with bride, groom, and priest at the center of the painting, a group of men beside Joseph and a group of women beside Mary, and the temple in the background, surrounded by steps leading up to it. But there are more differences—some of which are also more significant—than similarities between the two. In the first place, the main characters are reversed compared to Perugino's altarpiece, but it is the temple that really determines the superiority of Raphael's painting. While the master's large octagonal-shaped temple looms over the figures, the pupil's version is light and airy, with 16 sides giving it a sense of circularity, and the higher staircase providing a greater vertical dynamic. The characters also depend on this circular space, appearing to be arranged along a curve, rather than simply lined up, as in Perugino's painting. The effect is one of great harmony and balance, and it is further refined by another small detail representing a revolution in the depiction of figures: liberated from rigidity by Raphael's masterful brushstrokes, they display a new and unprecedented ease.

132 THE MARRIAGE OF THE VIRGIN *(OIL ON PANEL; 67 X 46 INCHES/170 X 118 CENTIMETERS), THE FIRST WORK BY THE URBINO MASTER RAPHAEL, WAS INSPIRED BY AN ALTARPIECE ON THE SAME THEME BY PERUGINO, NOW IN THE MUSÉE DES BEAUX-ARTS IN CAEN, FRANCE.*

Giorgione's *Tempest*

Standing before Giorgione's *Tempest* in the Gallerie dell'Accademia in Venice, it is essential to clear your mind for a moment, sweeping away all the hypotheses, conjectures, theories, and myths that have accompanied any reading of this painting for half a millennium. Then, as you approach the canvas, you can finally "enter into" the spirit of the picture—you can feel the air turning cool and the leaves rustling, moved by a sudden gust of wind and the coming storm. At the heart of the image is the lightning, captured at the instant it flashes, so that it transforms everything you see in the painting. The artist from Castelfranco Veneto, near Venice, was commissioned in the early 1500s by the nobleman Gabriele Vendramin, and the resulting painting stands out in its own right, above and beyond any presumed hidden allegorical meanings. For the first time in Renaissance painting, the landscape takes on a leading role, expressing the mood even more intensely than the figures. With his revolutionary use of tonal painting, which harmonizes the colors by nuancing them, Giorgione creates a kind of interconnectedness between the figures and the landscape, allowing the latter to become the protagonist. This effect is also achieved by the fact that the artist worked directly with his paints, without any preparatory drawing. The scene appears utterly dynamic and alive, as a vibrant whole: a characteristic that would mark all Venetian painting throughout the 16th century, beginning with Titian. Even today, the identities of the two individuals in the painting remain a mystery: the young half-nude woman captured in the act of breastfeeding her child and, to the left, a young man dressed in contemporary clothes, leaning on a stick and observing her—figures that appear to be close to each other, but are in fact separated by the course of a river. The town upon which the storm is about to descend is unknown, but it is often identified as Padua due to the buildings resembling the tower of the Castle of Ezzelino, the bridge of San Tommaso, and the dome of the Church of the Carmine.

134-135 *With Giorgione's Tempest (oil on canvas; 33 x 29 inches/83 x 73 centimeters), for the first time in Western art, landscape was no longer simply used as a background in a painting, but as a feature and an expression of a state of mind.*

Michelangelo Buonarroti's *Pietà*

The last canto of Dante's *Divine Comedy* begins with the words "Virgin mother, daughter of your son," and these must have been close to Michelangel's heart as he sculpted the Pietà between 1498 and 1499. His cultural education had taken place at the court of Lorenzo de' Medici, and in his early 20s the sculptor became a great admirer of the work of Dante, from which he drew much poetic inspiration. The face of the Madonna holding the lifeless body of Christ in her lap is portrayed as very youthful, the "daughter of her son," rather than that of an older woman, as was the custom of the time. The perfect features of the Virgin Mary and her son fuse together in a union of beauty, both physical and spiritual. The theme of the Pietà also deviates from the usual representations of the scene in Renaissance art; it takes its inspiration from devotional images, usually in wood, in the style known as "Vesperbild" (literally, Vespers image), which originated in Germany in the 14th century and was particularly widespread in northern Europe. Indeed, this geographic characteristic explains Michelangelo's unusual choice. The French Cardinal Jean de Bilhères, who commissioned the work, came to Rome to serve as Charles VIII's ambassador to Pope Alexander VI. The result is the famous masterpiece, housed in the first chapel of the right aisle in St. Peter's Basilica in Vatican City, the construction of which Michelangelo himself worked on from 1546 until his death in 1564. The most striking feature of the painting is the naturalness of Christ's pose as he lies dead in his mother's lap. Light hits the faces of both subjects and the rich drapery of the Virgin's veil brings to the work a translucent effect that makes the sculptures wax-like. Clearly visible on the sash of the Virgin Mary is the inscription "Michael. Angelus. Bonarotus. Florent. Faciebat." ("Michelangelo Buonarroti of Florence Created This"), the only known signature on any of his works. Legend has it that while mingling with the crowd who had come to admire his work, the artist heard it being attributed to the Lombard Cristoforo Solari, known as Il Gobbo, and thus engraved his own name in order to dispel any doubt.

136, 137 AND 138-139 *MICHELANGELO'S PIETÀ IN ST. PETER'S BASILICA WAS THE ONLY WORK THE ARTIST SIGNED. THE MASTERPIECE (17 FEET/5.17 METERS) WAS SCULPTED FROM A BLOCK OF MARBLE CHOSEN BY THE ARTIST FROM THE CARRARA QUARRIES.*

Michelangelo Buonarroti's *David*

It has been more than 500 years since Michelangelo completed his famous marble giant 17 feet (5.17 meters) high in 1504, originally destined to adorn one of the buttresses on Florence's Santa Maria del Fiore Cathedral, and still *David* continues to create scandal. The latest attempt to dress the sculpture, or rather, a copy of it, was in early 2013, when a life-size replica of the statue erected in a public park in Japan created such a stir that demands were made to clothe it. The same reaction was sparked among the ultra-Orthodox and Arab communities in Jerusalem by the copy given to the city by Florence, in celebration of the 3,000th anniversary of the city's conquest by King David. Things went more smoothly in London, when, in 1857, the umpteenth copy of the biblical hero was donated to Queen Victoria by the grand duke of Tuscany: she had a simple fig leaf added to it. Never has the maxim "Many enemies, much honor" been more true than in this case. The *David* that, since 1837, we have been admiring in the Tribuna at Florence's Accademia Gallery ("Galleria dell'Accademia"), built specifically to host the work, is universally recognized as the most important Renaissance sculpture, an incredible combination of physical strength—with the figure's athletic body and perfect musculature—and expressiveness, conveyed by the proud, menacing look of the youth ready to face the giant Goliath. Thanks to its sheer beauty—as Vasari wrote, *David* "carried off the palm from all other statues, modern or ancient"—and power, the statue immediately became a symbol of the New Republic that expelled the Medici from Florence in 1494. It is also why the statue was "diverted" from the cathedral for which it was originally destined, and relocated to the Piazza della Signoria, where one of the two Florentine copies of *David* stands today. The other copy, in bronze, stands triumphantly at the center of the Piazzale Michelangelo, the renowned square named after the sculptor, from where there is a panoramic view of Florence.

140 AND 141 *SCULPTED BETWEEN 1501 AND 1504, MICHELANGELO'S ORIGINAL DAVID WAS MOVED IN 1873 FROM THE PIAZZA DELLA SIGNORIA TO THE TRIBUNA OF THE ACCADEMIA GALLERY ("GALLERIA DELL'ACCADEMIA"), CONSTRUCTED EXPRESSLY TO HOUSE THE MARBLE GIANT.*

IONAS

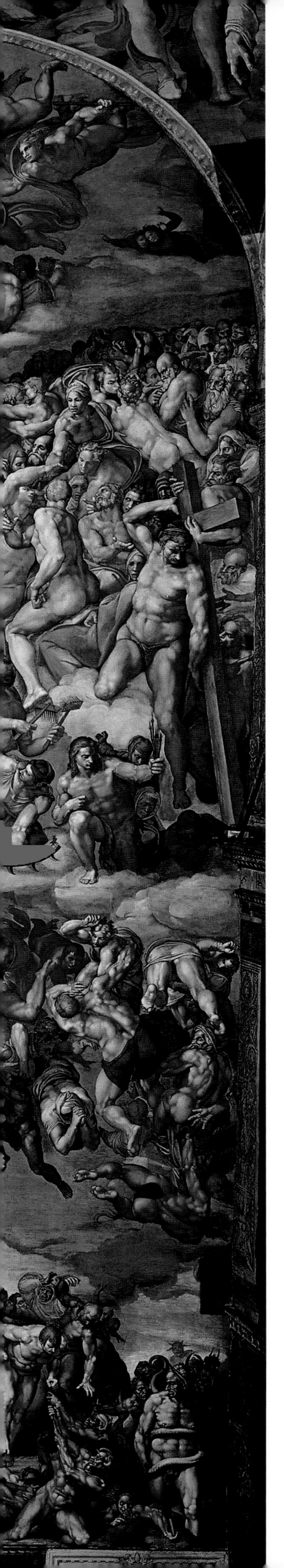

Michelangelo Buonarroti's Sistine Chapel

It's incredible but true, the decorations in the Sistine Chapel, admired each year by over 5 million visitors, were Michelangelo Buonarroti's first encounter with the technique of fresco. Donato Bramante was well aware of this when he mischievously put forward Michelangelo's name to Pope Julius II, in a thinly veiled attempt to discredit the artist, who until that point had distinguished himself as a skilled sculptor, and have the work passed to his friend Raphael. But talent, as we know, is unpredictable, and confronted with this new commission, Michelangelo succeeded in transferring the powerful modeling of his sculptures into painting form. The stories from the Book of Genesis, covering over 7,500 square feet (700 square meters) of the chapel's vault and linking with its 15th-century cycle of frescoes by Perugino, Botticelli, and Ghirlandaio, represented an exceptionally intense physical and creative challenge for Michelangelo. Working in complete solitude, between 1508 and 1512, he grappled with the task in an artistic struggle that produced over 400 figures, illustrating the biblical stories with a power that had never been seen before. The inauguration of the ceiling on All Saints' Day was a complete triumph, so that later Vasari would write: "This work has proved a veritable beacon to our art, of inestimable benefit to all painters, restoring light to a world that for centuries had been plunged into darkness." In 1537 Michelangelo was summoned again, this time by Pope Clement VII to paint his masterpiece *The Last Judgment* on the rear wall of the chapel. Combining the biblical prophecy with Dante's *Divine Comedy*, Michelangelo succeeded in constructing a monumental scene using only human bodies, depicting 391 figures of the damned and the redeemed, creating the same three-dimensional architectural effect as that used for the ceiling. When the work with its nude figures was revealed in 1541, in its position behind the holiest altar in Christianity, it was judged scandalous, to the extent that Daniele da Volterra (later branded "Il Braghettone," roughly, "the underpants man") was commissioned to "put the undergarments" onto Michelangelo's magnificent bodies.

142-143 *The Last Judgment, behind Christianity's most sacred altar, is Michelangelo Buonarroti's masterpiece. The artist painted the fresco on the rear wall of the Sistine Chapel between 1536 and 1541.*

144-145 *It took four years of hard work to complete the frescoes on the vault of the Sistine Chapel: (12,000 square feet/1,100 square meters) on which Michelangelo worked single-handedly from 1508.*

IOEL
ERITHRAEA

146 THE ORIGINAL SIN IS ONE OF THE NINE STORIES FROM THE BOOK OF GENESIS PAINTED ON THE VAULT. HERE ADAM AND EVE ARE TEMPTED BY AN ANTHROPOMORPHIC SERPENT BEFORE BEING DRIVEN OUT BY AN ANGEL.

147 THE FOURTH SCENE DEPICTED ON THE VAULT IS THE CREATION OF ADAM, THE MOST WELL-KNOWN DETAIL FROM THE SISTINE CHAPEL. GOD, SURROUNDED BY ANGELS, TRANSMITS THE BREATH OF LIFE INTO MAN, THROUGH THE EXTENDED FINGERS.

The Raphael Rooms at the Vatican Museums

Popes like to leave their mark on history. They have done so through the ages and continue to do so today. It was certainly the case with Julius II, who was pope between 1503 and 1513 and the greatest patron of the arts the church has ever known. It is Julius II, born Giuliano della Rovere, and his desire to avoid confrontation with his predecessor, Alexander VI, whom we have to thank for the Raphael Rooms ("Stanze di Raffaello"), one of the most interesting parts of the Vatican museums. He chose not to live in the Borgias' apartments, instead moving to the second floor of the papal palace, where, on the advice of Bramante, he entrusted Raphael, the artist from Urbino, with the decoration of four rooms. He completed the task in 1520, the year of his death, with the assistance of several pupils. He was working on the commission at the same time as Michelangelo was painting the Sistine Chapel, and in the most famous fresco in the papal apartments, *The School of Athens*, Heraclitus is portrayed with the features of Michelangelo, an ironic tribute paid by Raphael to his rival. The painting is housed in the Room of the Signatura ("Stanza della Segnatura"), which was originally used by the pope as a library. The room's four paintings depict distinct branches of knowledge, and represent the three greatest categories of the human spirit: Truth, Good, and Beauty. Portraits of Julius II's contemporaries in ancient settings, placed among figures of the past in anachronistic fashion, are depicted in several frescoes in his apartments; Julius himself is shown on the *seda gestatoria* (ceremonial throne) witnessing *The Expulsion of Heliodorus from the Temple*, a biblical episode that gives its name to another of the rooms. This fresco, along with those portraying *The Mass of Bolsena* and *The Deliverance of St. Peter,* was intended to reveal the protection given by God to the church under threat. Another pope, Leo X, commissioned the decoration of the Room of the Fire in the Borgo ("Stanza dell'Incendio di Borgo"), which depicts the lives of two other popes, each of whom bears the features of the reigning pope. Giulio Romano, Raphael's favorite pupil, helped to complete the frescoes and is responsible for the four episodes from the life of Constantine that adorn the Hall of Constantine ("Sala di Constantino"), along with Tommaso Laureti's *Triumph of the Christian Religion.*

148 *In the Stanza di Eliodoro, one of the Raphael Rooms, Raphael painted the Deliverance of St. Peter (detail shown here) to show God's protection of the Church under threat with the liberation of St. Peter, the first pope.*

149 *Perugino, Raphael's teacher, was commissioned to paint the vault of the Stanza dell'Incendio del Borgo, another of the Raphael Rooms, by Pope Julius II, when it was still used to hold meetings of the Holy See's highest court.*

150-151 *The School of Athens in the Stanza della Segnatura is one of the greatest masterpieces of the Vatican museums. Ancient Greek philosophers Plato and Aristotle are depicted at the center of the fresco.*

Titian Vecellio's *Sacred and Profane Love*

152-153 *One of the great symbolic works of the Galleria Borghese,* Sacred and Profane Love *(oil on canvas; 46 x 110 inches/118 x 279 centimeters) was presumably acquired in 1608 by Cardinal Scipione Borghese to enrich his extensive collection.*

In 1899, the Rothschild bankers offered a remarkable 4 million liras (about US$ 22,675,000, adjusted for inflation) for the masterpiece by Titian (Tiziano Vecellio) *Sacred and Profane Love*, a key work in the Galleria Borghese's collection. The figure is astronomical when compared to the amount offered by the same Rothschilds for the entire Villa Borghese, including works of art: "only" 3,600,000 liras (about US$ 20 million). On the other hand, executed by the great Venetian painter for the wedding of Niccolò Aurelio and Laura Bagarotto, as can be seen from the coat of arms painted on the sarcophagus at the center of the picture, the painting is among the most studied and discussed works in the history of art. The true identities of the women portrayed are not known and even the title of the work represents yet another (moralizing) reading of the subject. The painting depicts two women who have similar features, but who nevertheless are in striking contrast to each other. The woman on the left is dressed in what might be a wedding gown, suggested by its white color, the belt, gloves, and myrtle wreath—a symbol of conjugal love—and also the washbowl standing on the rim of the sarcophagus on which the woman is seated, probably an item from the wedding trousseau. Behind her, a pair of rabbits, symbolizing fertility, stands out against a landscape dominated by a fortified city at dawn. The play of contrasts continues on the opposite side of the sarcophagus, where a nude woman is seated, partially draped in a garment of red—in the color that would henceforth be identified in painting as "Titian red"—contrasting with the whiteness of the clothed woman. Even the background changes completely, with a bucolic landscape at sunset materializing behind the beautiful young nude woman. Between the two women, Cupid stirs the water, symbolizing life, transforming the sarcophagus, referencing death, into a fountain, thus becoming a sort of intermediary between heaven and earth, between divine love and terrestrial love, as represented by the two female figures.

Caravaggio's *Basket of Fruit*

154-155 Caravaggio's *Basket of Fruit* (oil on canvas; 18 x 24 inches/47 x 62 centimeters), the greatest of all still lifes, was donated by Cardinal del Monte to Federico Borromeo, founder of the historic library, the Biblioteca Ambrosiana, where the work is still exhibited.

"I wanted to put another similar basket alongside it, but as no one had been able to achieve the incomparable beauty and excellence of this one, it remained alone." Thus wrote Cardinal Federico Borromeo in 1625 in his book *Musaeum Bibliothecae Ambrosianae*, referring to Caravaggio's *Basket of Fruit*, which had been given to the cardinal by Francesco Maria del Monte a few years earlier. It became a part of Borromeo's private collection and shortly thereafter found a place in the new Pinacoteca Ambrosiana ("Ambrosian Art Gallery"), where, now considered the greatest still life in Italian painting, it can still be seen today. It is difficult, in fact, to find a picture that could justifiably be placed alongside this one, so brilliantly has it been painted by Michelangelo Merisi da Caravaggio in the late 1500s, the only remaining still life by the Lombard master. The revolutionary idea that guided the hand of the artist was to take the genre of still life seriously, which until then had been considered of only minor importance. According to Caravaggio, "it took as much manufacturing to produce a good painting of flowers as it did to make one of figures," a conviction that he demonstrated so ably in this painting. Caravaggio's basket of fruit, which has been inspiring still life painters for some 400 years, impresses with its exacting adherence to reality and can easily hold its own against any portrait from the same era. The detail is so precise and meticulous that, even though it depicts fruit that is less than perfect, the painting evokes life far more than it does death. You can almost smell the aroma of the apples and pears. Nature is revealed in all its spontaneity by the light that pervades the image and comes to rest on each grape, imparting a delicate transparency, and on the worm-eaten apple and the wrinkled skin of the figs. Even the leaves, which become ever drier as the gaze shifts to the right, seem to remind the viewer of the transience of life, the fleeting nature of beauty. The full extent of Caravaggio's genius is evident here as he illustrates, using a simple basket resting upon a table, the precariousness of our existence.

Paolo Veronese's *Feast in the House of Levi*

156-157 *Paolo Veronese completed the painting later known under the title* The Feast in the House of Levi *18 x 42 feet (5.55 x 12.80 meters) when the Counter-Reformation was at its height, and was summoned before the tribunal of the Roman Catholic Inquisition to respond to the charge of heresy.*

On July 18, 1573, the court of the Inquisition declared Paolo Caliari, known as Veronese, a heretic. Summoned to the Chapel of San Teodoro, the seat of the Inquisition in Venice, the painter had just completed the large painting commissioned by the Dominicans of the convent of Santi Giovanni e Paolo in Venice. His work was to replace the *Last Supper* by Titian, which had been destroyed in a fire. However, the prior of the convent did not care too much for Veronese's vision of the *Last Supper*, and when he requested a number of changes, the artist flatly refused to make them. The painting, although perfect in its technical composition, was deemed to be irreverent, if not wholly blasphemous. The scene depicted had little to do with the traditional iconography of the *Last Supper*, not least the setting itself: a lavish palace in the style of Palladio. A sumptuous banquet has been set out in a loggia framed by three arches. At the center is the figure of Christ, accompanied by St. Peter and St. John, but the other apostles, even Judas, are absent. A very mixed crowd of people mingles, apparently paying no attention to the Eucharist supper. As if on a stage, a veritable retinue of extraordinary figures is present, including jesters, dogs, pages, servants, soldiers, and people in 16th-century costume. Veronese's response to the inquisitors when they questioned such choices was breathtaking: "We painters take the same liberties as poets and madmen." Veronese's subsequent strategy was both limited and effective—he made no changes to the work itself, he simply changed the title. Henceforth, the canvas, still on display in the Gallerie dell'Accademia in Venice, was known as *The Feast in the House of Levi*, a depiction of the dinner from the Gospel of Luke, organized for Jesus by the wealthy publican Levi. The banquet ended with the conversion of the master of the house, and like Veronese and his painting, in the biblical story Levi changed his name from then on to Matthew.

Gian Lorenzo Bernini's *Apollo and Daphne*

The incredible vitality in Bernini's *Apollo and Daphne* is astounding. The work—commissioned by Cardinal Scipione Borghese and carried out between 1622 and 1625 by the sculptor who was barely 25—captures all the energy of motion as if it were a snapshot in time. Daphne, immortalized in the act of metamorphosing into a laurel tree to escape Apollo's love, wears an expression of disbelief mixed with desperation. With her forward-leaning posture, Daphne appears to be supported by her feet but they are transforming into roots; Apollo, who has just caught up with her, places his hand on one of her hips only to find it has just turned into bark, while profuse and delicate laurel leaves sprout from the nymph's fingers. With great virtuosity, Bernini succeeds in transforming Ovid's words into physical reality, carving a statue of the story from the *Metamorphoses*, from which he took inspiration. This sculptural group, along with Bernini's other three Borghese commissions, his *Aeneas, Anchises, and Ascanius*, *The Rape of Proserpina*, and his *David*, can still be seen at the very site for which they were commissioned, the Villa Borghese, the cardinal's "villa of delights." The story Bernini tells here develops as the sculpture, its creator, and the viewer meet. The dramatic action in *Apollo and Daphne* unfolds before the admiring gaze of the observer, an aspect that was accentuated even more when the sculpture was situated to the side of the room adjacent to the chapel, on a low base. In this position, the viewer would first encounter Apollo from behind, as the god was nearing the end of his race to reach the object of his desire, with the drapery on his form still evoking the impression of movement. Then, as the viewer moves forward, around the statue, the action of the group takes center stage, and is finally reflected in the dramatic expressions on the protagonists' faces. Lower down on the base, a couplet inscribed on a scroll justifies the presence of this pagan image in the house of a cardinal: "He who loves to chase after fleeting forms of entertainment finds himself, in the end, with bitter leaves and berries in hand." The words were written by Maffeo Barberini (later Pope Urban VIII), an *excusatio non petita* ("unrequested excuse"), leading the viewer to a Christian (and moralizing) reading of Bernini's masterpiece.

158 AND 159 *AS THOUGH CAPTURED IN A SNAPSHOT, BERNINI IMMORTALIZED THE METAMORPHOSIS OF THE NYMPH DAPHNE AS SHE IS PURSUED BY APOLLO, A TRANSFORMATION THAT INVOLVES EVEN THE MARBLE, WHICH, IN THE HANDS OF THE SCULPTOR, TURNS INTO HAIR, BARK, AND LEAVES.*

Antonio Canova's *Pauline Bonaparte*

"Camillo, I want to ask a favor of you... I know that once in a while you allow someone to see my marble statue. I would prefer you not to do this anymore, because the sculpture's nudity borders on indecency. It was created for your own pleasure, and since now that is no longer the case, it is right for it to remain hidden from the sight of others." So wrote Napoleon's younger sister, Pauline Bonaparte, to her husband, Prince Borghese, on January 2, 1818. However, it is as if these words had never been uttered, or rather, had never been written: today nearly 2,000 visitors line up daily at the Galleria Borghese to admire the marble statue that "seems like flesh and blood," sculpted between 1805 and 1808 by Antonio Canova. Commissioned by Pauline's husband, the sculptor from Possagno had portrayed Pauline, seminude and lying elegantly on a chaise longue, in the (nonexistent) garb of *Venus Victrix* ("Venus Victorious"), arousing scandal and surprise among the aristocratic circles of Rome. By deifying Princess Borghese, as he had previously done with her brother by portraying him as *Mars the Peacemaker*, Canova celebrated the splendor of the Bonaparte family. At the same time, to an extent, he also "indemnified" the Borghese collection, since shortly before its archaeological collection had been deprived of 344 pieces, donated by Camillo himself free of charge to his brother-in-law Napoleon; today they form the heart of the Greco-Roman collection at the Louvre. To offer the viewer a better perspective on what even today is considered the pinnacle of neoclassicism, Canova also installed a hidden mechanism in the supporting platform that allowed the statue to rotate. Given the display position that Canova's work occupies inside the Galleria Borghese, this facility is no longer needed. Since 1889, the *Venus Victrix* has occupied the center of the first room in the gallery, referred to as the Pauline Room, where it can be admired easily from every angle and the luminosity and softness of the work can be appreciated, effects that Canova obtained by applying a thin layer of wax to enhance the modeling of the marble.

160-161 *Canova sculpted the 25-year-old Pauline Borghese from a single block of Carrara marble. The life-sized neoclassical sculpture 36 x 79 inches (92 x 200 centimeters) dating from 1889 is one of the Galleria Borghese's most iconic works.*

Landscapes and Villages: Italy's Great Natural Theater

"The landscape is the breath of our soul." As poetic as it is true, this is how Oscar winner Roberto Benigni chose to comment on Article 9 of the Italian Constitution: "The Republic promotes the development of culture and of scientific and technical research. It safeguards natural landscape and the historical and artistic heritage of the Nation." It was the first constitution in the world to introduce among its fundamental principles a proposition dedicated to preserving the landscape, since, again according to Benigni, the Italian landscape "is present in the eyes, in the mind, and in the memory of the whole world, in the greatest works of painting and literature." The link between cultural heritage and that of the natural beauty of the countryside is very close and has marked the Italian peninsula profoundly throughout the centuries, shaping its identity. The peninsula's cultural heritage and language were both "Italian" before Italy was even born as a unified country in 1861, as travelers on the Grand Tour well knew—the essential educational journey undertaken, from the late 1600s, by young aristocrats from all over Europe. And before them, in the Middle Ages, it was pilgrims who would travel the country, making their way along the Via Francigena, toward Rome, to pay tribute to the tomb of the Apostle Peter.

Our journey through the sublime Italian landscapes aims to recover the sense of wonder and amazement that the travelers of the past felt. It showcases the open-air museum of contemporary Italy, where man and nature have come together to form the immeasurable charm and huge variety of this wonderful country.

The beauty of the mountains is dizzying. Some of them mark geographic boundaries: Monte Rosa, in whose shadow the culture and traditions of the Walser still survive today; Monte Bianco, on whose walls, from 1786, the most important pages in mountaineering history have been written; Monte Cervino, the mountain that has become an icon, thanks to its pyramid shape and its isolation in relation to other peaks. The Dolomites range have their own magical beauty: a symphony of steep mountain slopes, combined with rocky spires, belfries, steeples, towers, and jagged teeth, formed over the centuries by the ravages of climate, a natural masterpiece that Le Corbusier defined as "the most beautiful piece of architecture in the world."

The lakes of Italy, the most numerous in Mediterranean Europe, are entire landscapes in miniature: micro-regions of water and mountain, where man has left his mark in the exquisite villas reflected in the waters of Lake Como between Cernobbio and Bellagio, or on the shores of Lake Garda, where the poet Gabriele d'Annunzio—who understood about landscape—built the Vittoriale degli Italiani, the magnificent estate where he spent the last part of his life. This landscape has inspired many writers, including the poet and novelist Cesare Pavese, much of whose work features the Langhe region in northern Italy, his own "inner geography." This vista of vineyards and farms, bordering Monferrat and Roero and embracing an ocean of rolling hills, recalls, by contrast, another sea, the Ligurian Sea that laps the shores of the Cinque Terre, where vines are cultivated on terraced hills overlooking the glinting waves, leaving barely enough room for the five villages now protected by UNESCO as World Heritage Sites for their cultural value and natural beauty.

Nature's encounter with man again characterizes the region in the Itria Valley, creating a striking landscape reminiscent of the three colors of the Italian flag: the dazzling white of the trulli, the typical lime-washed farmhouses; the green of the olive trees and the vines; and the red of the fertile earth in which they flourish. The Sassi di Matera, on the other hand, exerts a very different kind of charm. An ancient city excavated out of the local tuff, it has been inhabited continuously since the Paleolithic period to the present day. Another important encounter occurred here, this time between the cinema and the Italian landscape, a combination that has generated some consummate cinematic masterpieces, such as The Gospel According to St. Matthew by Pier Paolo Pasolini, turning the Italian peninsula into a unique film set for cinema auteur and forming a central thread for discovering other beautiful parts of the country. Soviet director Andrei Tarkovsky filmed some unforgettable images at the extraordinary Bagno Vignoni in Val d'Orcia, where, in the constant pursuit of beauty, art and landscape come together in perfect union.

The natural landscape featured by another great master, Michelangelo Antonioni, in the film L'Avventura, is charged with metaphorical significance. The director's camera explores the lunar-like surface of Lisca Bianca in the Aeolian Islands, turning the rocky volcanic reef into an interior landscape. Italy's ravishing offshore islands are the peninsula's rebellious daughters, beautiful but difficult to tame. Even Capri, the most famous and well known, continues to both move and astonish visitors with its natural beauty, its cliff top paths seemingly suspended over the sea. Among these scenic wonders, the Maddalena Archipelago off the northeast coast of Sardinia is the quintessence of Mediterranean beauty, while the Pontine Islands of Ponza and Ventotene have been transformed from places of confinement and exile into destinations of choice for those seeking the tranquility and color that is so hard to find elsewhere.

For those in search of traditional breathtaking views, the Amalfi Coast does not disappoint, captivating all those who visit. Flights of steps lead upward between winding roads, and balconies and rocky promontories look out over the sea, making this enchanting stretch of coastline very special, with its unique combination of natural and architectural beauty; it is almost as difficult to negotiate as it is rewarding to visit. Portofino, with the world's most beautiful town square, is equally wonderful, as is San Gimignano, a medieval Manhattan characterized by its mighty tower-houses that cast long shadows. Once again, it is the harmony between the urban space and the surrounding countryside that inspires admiration and wonder: encapsulating the magical quality of the Italian landscape, which bewitches visitors today, just as it did in centuries past, ensuring it remains "in the eyes, in the mind, and in the memory of the whole world."

164-165 The Rosengarten ("Il Catinaccio") and the Vajolet Towers ("Torri del Vajolet") form a backdrop for the Larsec crags ("Dirupi di Larsec"), the cradle of mountaineering in the Val di Fassa. These peaks are noted for the particular coloring they take on at sunrise and sunset.

165 The spectacular rock spires of the Pale di San Martino constitute one of the nine mountain groups registered as a Natural World Heritage Site by UNESCO.

The Magical Peaks of the Dolomites

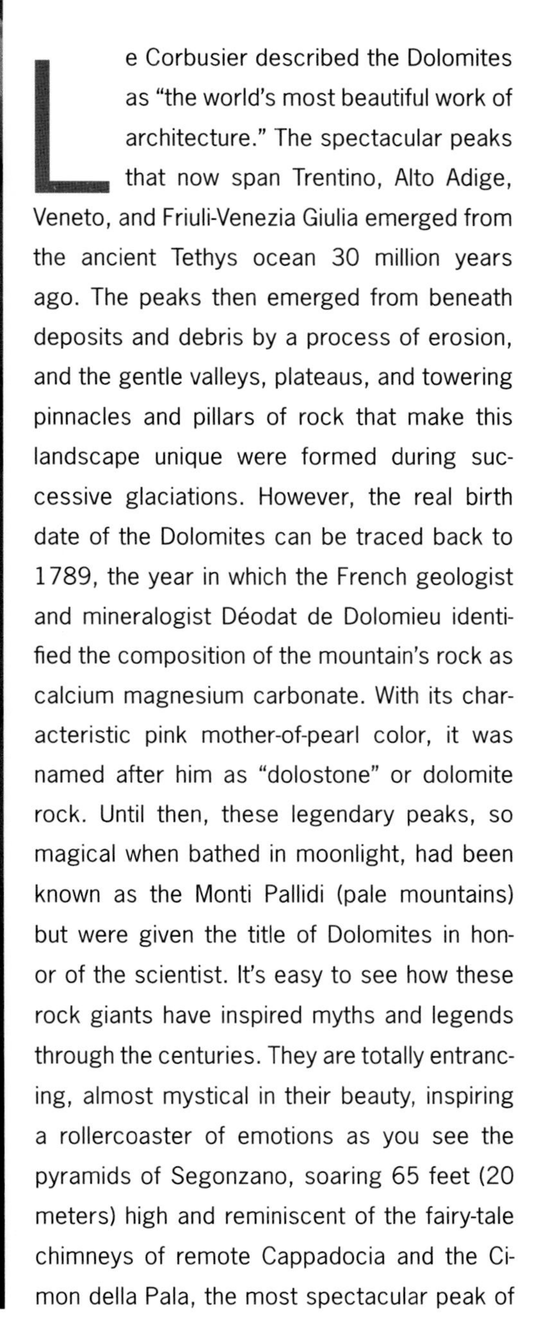

Le Corbusier described the Dolomites as "the world's most beautiful work of architecture." The spectacular peaks that now span Trentino, Alto Adige, Veneto, and Friuli-Venezia Giulia emerged from the ancient Tethys ocean 30 million years ago. The peaks then emerged from beneath deposits and debris by a process of erosion, and the gentle valleys, plateaus, and towering pinnacles and pillars of rock that make this landscape unique were formed during successive glaciations. However, the real birth date of the Dolomites can be traced back to 1789, the year in which the French geologist and mineralogist Déodat de Dolomieu identified the composition of the mountain's rock as calcium magnesium carbonate. With its characteristic pink mother-of-pearl color, it was named after him as "dolostone" or dolomite rock. Until then, these legendary peaks, so magical when bathed in moonlight, had been known as the Monti Pallidi (pale mountains) but were given the title of Dolomites in honor of the scientist. It's easy to see how these rock giants have inspired myths and legends through the centuries. They are totally entrancing, almost mystical in their beauty, inspiring a rollercoaster of emotions as you see the pyramids of Segonzano, soaring 65 feet (20 meters) high and reminiscent of the fairy-tale chimneys of remote Cappadocia and the Cimon della Pala, the most spectacular peak of the Pale di San Martino group, just above the Rolle Pass. The landscape becomes sublime at the Tre Cime di Lavaredo, three distinctive peaks in the Sexten Dolomites that are a paradise for both geologists and mountaineers, offering breathtaking views from Punta Rocca of Marmolada, the highest peak in the Dolomites at 10,968 feet (3343 meters). In 2011, the highest terrace in the eastern Italian Alps was inaugurated, providing a front row seat for magnificent views of Sella, Sassolungo, Pelmo, and Civetta. To enjoy the wonderful spectacle of sunrise and sunset on Marmolada and Tofane, the Lagazuoi refuge is the place to head for, high above the Falzarego Pass, halfway between Cortina d'Ampezzo, the "Queen of the Dolomites," and the Badia valley, where Michelin-starred restaurants and beauty spas await.

166-167 *In the Alta Val Badia in the heart of the Dolomites, where the towns of Colfosco, Corvara, La Villa, San Cassiano, Pedraces, San Leonardo, and La Val are located, efforts have been focused in recent years on the quality of hospitality.*

167 *The Langkofel (or "Sassolungo") at 10,436 feet (3,181 meters) is the highest peak of the massif that extends between the Sella Group and the Rosengarten Group, forming the border between the Val Gardena and the Val di Fassa.*

168-169 *The east face of Monte Rosa is the highest in the Alps, towering 15,092 feet (4,600 meters) at the head of Valle Anzasca, the valley that is home to the ancient Walser village of Macugnaga.*

Monte Rosa and the Walser People

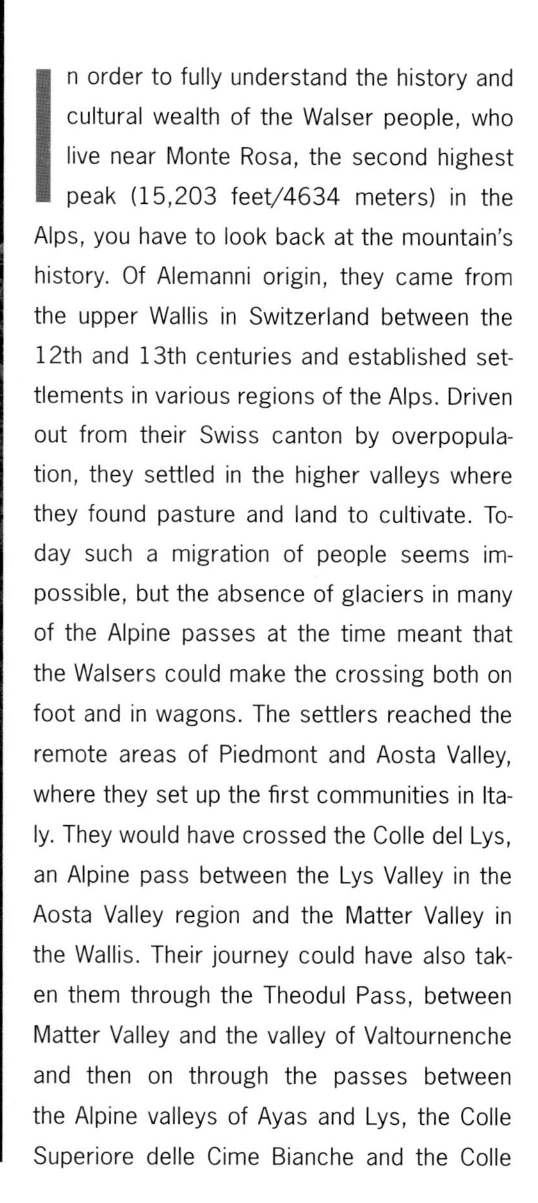

In order to fully understand the history and cultural wealth of the Walser people, who live near Monte Rosa, the second highest peak (15,203 feet/4634 meters) in the Alps, you have to look back at the mountain's history. Of Alemanni origin, they came from the upper Wallis in Switzerland between the 12th and 13th centuries and established settlements in various regions of the Alps. Driven out from their Swiss canton by overpopulation, they settled in the higher valleys where they found pasture and land to cultivate. Today such a migration of people seems impossible, but the absence of glaciers in many of the Alpine passes at the time meant that the Walsers could make the crossing both on foot and in wagons. The settlers reached the remote areas of Piedmont and Aosta Valley, where they set up the first communities in Italy. They would have crossed the Colle del Lys, an Alpine pass between the Lys Valley in the Aosta Valley region and the Matter Valley in the Wallis. Their journey could have also taken them through the Theodul Pass, between Matter Valley and the valley of Valtournenche and then on through the passes between the Alpine valleys of Ayas and Lys, the Colle Superiore delle Cime Bianche and the Colle della Bettaforca. The Walser then reached the valleys of Valsesia, Anzasca, Ossola, and Formazza. Wherever they went, they worked tirelessly, draining and reclaiming vast areas of land, and establishing small settlements, several of which became the towns of Alagna, Gressoney, and Macugnaga where the Walser culture has been most preserved; examples of their architecture in wood and stone still charm visitors today. Equally fascinating for those interested in ethnography are the people living in the various settlements of Monte Rosa. Even the name of the language, which has its origins in an archaic form of German, varies between locations. In Gressoney-St. Jean, people speak *titsch*, whereas down at Issime, the dialect is *töitschu*, known in the towns of Alagna, Rima, and Rimella as *titzschu*. It is a real tower of Babel, and this diversity is also reflected in the Walser costumes, with their wonderfully diverse colors and designs.

The Walsertreffen, a large meeting held every three years at one of the historic settlements in the Alps, at which the age-old partnership between these ancient communities is revitalized, provides an opportunity to see their different dress and customs.

170-171 The Regina Margherita refuge, constructed in 1893, is on the Signalkuppe ("Punta Gnifetti"), the highest peak in the Sesia Valley 14,941 feet (4,554 meters). In addition to being a mountain refuge, it also houses an important physical-meteorological observatory.

171 There is a notable Walser presence in the Alagna area, in the Lombardy region. Traveling from Macugnaga through the Turlo Pass, the Walser people (of Germanic origin) arrived in the Sesia Valley between the 12th and 13th centuries.

172-173 *The walls of the Matterhorn ("Monte Cervino") are oriented according to the points of the compass. To the north, Cervino looks toward Zermatt in Switzerland, to the east, it looks on the Gorner Glacier, to the south, the Italian alpine resort of Breuil-Cervinia, and to the west, it faces the mountain Dent d'Hérens.*

The Matterhorn: Challenge and Conquest

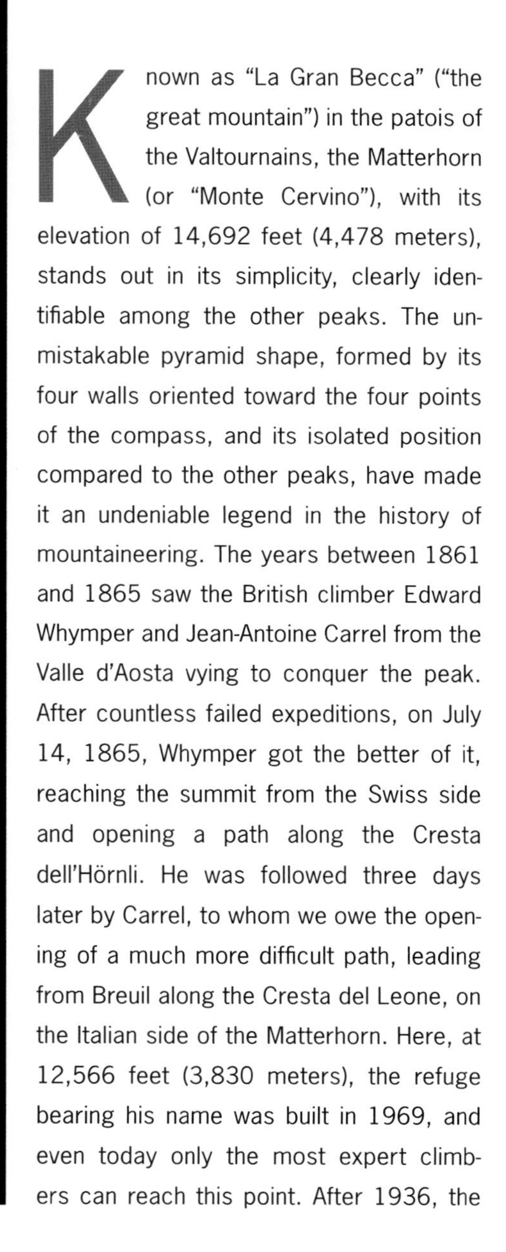

Known as "La Gran Becca" ("the great mountain") in the patois of the Valtournains, the Matterhorn (or "Monte Cervino"), with its elevation of 14,692 feet (4,478 meters), stands out in its simplicity, clearly identifiable among the other peaks. The unmistakable pyramid shape, formed by its four walls oriented toward the four points of the compass, and its isolated position compared to the other peaks, have made it an undeniable legend in the history of mountaineering. The years between 1861 and 1865 saw the British climber Edward Whymper and Jean-Antoine Carrel from the Valle d'Aosta vying to conquer the peak. After countless failed expeditions, on July 14, 1865, Whymper got the better of it, reaching the summit from the Swiss side and opening a path along the Cresta dell'Hörnli. He was followed three days later by Carrel, to whom we owe the opening of a much more difficult path, leading from Breuil along the Cresta del Leone, on the Italian side of the Matterhorn. Here, at 12,566 feet (3,830 meters), the refuge bearing his name was built in 1969, and even today only the most expert climbers can reach this point. After 1936, the terrain of the Matterhorn saw a different kind of conquest, following Breuil's transformation from mountain pasture to ski resort, which began with the construction of the first cable car between Breuil and Plan Maison. It continued a few years later with the extension up to Plateau Rosa at 11,417 feet (3,480 meters), where the cable car arrives today, connecting the Cime Bianche stations (9,219 feet/2,810 meters) with Testa Grigia on the western border of the glacier. Upon arrival at the station, you can see all the great peaks exceeding 13,000 feet (4000 meters), from the Matterhorn to Mont Blanc, from Gran Paradiso to Monte Rosa, as well as the Swiss peaks of the Valais canton, and as far as Monte Viso. And the show goes on—on skis—along the 100 miles (160 kilometers) of the 66 ski runs of the Breuil-Cervinia to Valtournenche area, which total 224 miles (360 kilometers) if added to those of Zermatt. It is one of the most extensive ski "merry-go-rounds" in the Alps, having among its flagship runs the famous Ventina: 7 miles (11 kilometers) of breathtakingly beautiful views leading from Plateau Rosa down into the village of Cervinia (6,727 feet/2,050 meters).

The Snowcapped Mont Blanc Massif

Reopened in 2013 following restoration, the Museo Alpino Duca degli Abruzzi ("Duke of Abruzzi Alpine Museum"), built by Prince Luigi Amedeo of Savoy in 1929, is the perfect place to begin an approach to Mont Blanc. The small exhibition space housed in the Casa delle Guide at Courmayeur tells the story of the passionate relationship that has long existed, and continues to thrive, between man and the highest mountain in the Alps—indeed in all of Western Europe (15,780 feet/4,810 meters). It is no coincidence that Italy's first company of guides was formed here in 1850, second only to the one founded in Chamonix, the French "capital" of Mont Blanc. At 22 miles (36 kilometers) long and over 9 miles (15 kilometers) wide, the mountain extends deep into the Graian Alps and only reveals itself at the last moment upon arrival in Courmayeur, until then remaining hidden by the other minor peaks, which are quickly forgotten once the perennially snowy massif is finally glimpsed. Some of the highest walls of the Alps are located here, such as the Dente del Gigante, the Grandes Jorasses, and the Aiguille Noire de Peuterey, rising from Val Veny, one of the two valleys that open out at the foot of the massif and initially run along the Brenva Glacier, considered to be the highest icefall in the Alps. The ski area is located in Val Veny, linked with that of Checrouit, from where one can explore over 60 miles (100 kilometers) of mountain ski runs. The other valley that forms the eastern border with Mont Blanc, Val Ferret, at the feet of the Grandes Jorasses, is decidedly gentler, and a favorite destination for hikers in summer and cross-country skiers in winter, who all enjoy the fine trails starting from the small village of Planpincieux. Without too much effort, visitors can conquer the roof of Europe simply by taking a cable car, starting from La Palud (4,347 feet/1,325 meters), to the panoramic stopping point at Le Pavillon (7,129 feet/2,173 meters), near the Giardino Botanico Alpino Saussurea, Europe's highest botanical gardens, which collects and showcases natural species of flora from Mont Blanc and offers a wonderful view of the surrounding mountains and valleys.

174 The Mont Blanc ("Monte Bianco") massif includes some of the highest peaks in the Alpine system, such as the Aiguille Noire de Peuterey, which rises an impressive 12,379 feet (3,773 meters) from the meadows of Val Veny.

174-175 The Mur de la Côte and the peak of Mont Blanc 15,781 feet (4,810 meters) as they appear from the nearby the Col de la Brenva. The first climbers to reach the summit were Michel Paccard and Jacques Balmat, in 1786.

176-177 The eye-catching profile of the Dente del Gigante (13,169 feet/4,014 meters) is to be found in the northern part of the Mont Blanc massif, between Italy and France. This challenging peak is part of the history of mountaineering.

177 From the Aiguille de Rochefort 13,127 feet (4,001 meters), which connects the base ("the gum") of the Dente del Gigante ("Dent du Géant") with the Col des Grandes Jorasses, you can see one of the most spectacular panoramas of the entire Monte Bianco massif.

Palmanova:
Star of the Show

A star built to combat a crescent moon. The history behind the origins of Palmanova sounds rather like a conflict between celestial bodies. It was fear of a Turkish invasion that led to the birth of one of the most significant examples of the Renaissance concept of the ideal city. Fearing an invasion from the east, the Republic of Venice, La Serenissima, decided to construct an impregnable city-fortress, quite unlike any that had gone before it, entrusting its design to architect Vincenzo Scamozzi of Vicenza. On October 7, 1593, the anniversary of the victory of the Catholic maritime states over the Ottoman Empire at the Battle of Lepanto, the first stone was laid for what would be a geometrically perfect city: a nine-pointed star emerging from a circle of fortifications around 4.5 miles (7 kilometers) long, surrounded entirely by a moat and a second row of bastions, to which a third curtain wall was added later by Napoleon. The number three and its multiples recur frequently in elements of the city's construction: the nine points of the star, three circles of walls, and three access gates ("Porta Udine," "Porta Cividale," "Porta Aquileia"). Of the eight radial streets, six major roads converge in the hexagonal central square, the Piazza d'Armi or Piazza Grande, at the center of which is a six-sided base of Istrian stone, from which a tall flagpole rises. The best way to take in the geometry of this fascinating "war machine" is from above. From the ground, in fact, Palmanova is deliberately invisible, being built on the plain below the line of the horizon, remote from hills and mountains, in order to remain concealed from possible invaders. But ironically, as fate would have it, no invaders ever arrived during the 16th century, nor even later, when numerous barracks were established at Palmanova ready to defend the eastern border. Vacated after the fall of the Berlin wall, the military buildings are now playing a major role in the town's rebirth, through careful redevelopment, such as the former Montesanto barracks and the Napoleonic gunpowder magazine, which are being refurbished as exhibition space and to hold cultural events.

178-179 *The best way to fully appreciate Palmanova is from above. The heart of the Friulian city is Piazza d'Armi, so called because the military superintendent for the Venetian Republic would assemble soldiers here for military exercises.*

180-181 *Torbole is situated on the northern tip of Lake Garda, in Trentino, at the foot of Monte Baldo. Thanks to the winds that blow over the lake, known as the Ora and Peler, this is one of Europe's most popular destinations for windsurfers.*

181 *The crenellated walls of the Della Scala fortress in Sirmione seem to rise directly out of the lake; the towns people live in close proximity to the water. The castle was built in the 13th century by Mastino della Scala.*

Lake Garda: A Mediterranean Illusion

A remnant of the Mediterranean that ended up in the heart of northern Italy, bordering the regions of Lombardy, Veneto, and Trentino-Alto Adige, this lake is particularly popular with German, British, Belgian, and Dutch visitors. It is Italy's largest lake, extending over 143 square miles (370 square kilometers) and boasting a surprisingly diverse shoreline of almost 100 miles (158 kilometers). To the north, Benaco, as the lake was known in Roman times, projects into the surrounding landscape like an inland fjord, with the steep slopes of Monte Baldo rising on one side. However, toward the south, the mountains are lower and the lake becomes more of a sea as it flows into the embrace of rolling morainal hills. Thanks to Lake Garda's temperate Mediterranean climate, it has its very own rivieras—the Riviera dei Limoni, the western stretch of shoreline between the towns of Limone and Salò, and the Riviera degli Olivi, the eastern shore, home to olive trees for many centuries.

The climate has allowed the spontaneous growth of Mediterranean vegetation that blends palms, magnolias, and bougainvilleas with holm oaks, laurels, and cypresses, like those at Punta San Vigilio on the Verona side of the lake. This is perhaps the most romantic part of Lake Garda, visited in the past by such famous figures as British statesman Winston Churchill, and actors Vivien Leigh and Laurence Olivier, and where the 16th-century Villa Guarienti is located, one of the most beautiful residences on the lake. However, the most famous and popular of the many villas remains Vittoriale degli Italiani, the residence and monument on the Gardone Riviera where Gabriele D'Annunzio spent the final years of his life. It reflects the complex personality of the Italian writer, whose nickname was "The Prophet." It is to the family of another poet, Catullus, that the Roman villa now known as the Grotto of Catullus belonged. The ruins are located at the end of the Sirmione peninsula on the southern shore of the lake. The area has been renowned for its spas since 1898, due to the presence of its sulfurous and salso-bromo-iodic waters, with their recognized therapeutic properties. To the north is the area to which sports lovers head; it is here that Garda transforms into a wind tunnel, making it particularly popular among windsurfers, who find the breezes and waves at Malcesine, Riva del Garda, and Torbole ideal for their board sports.

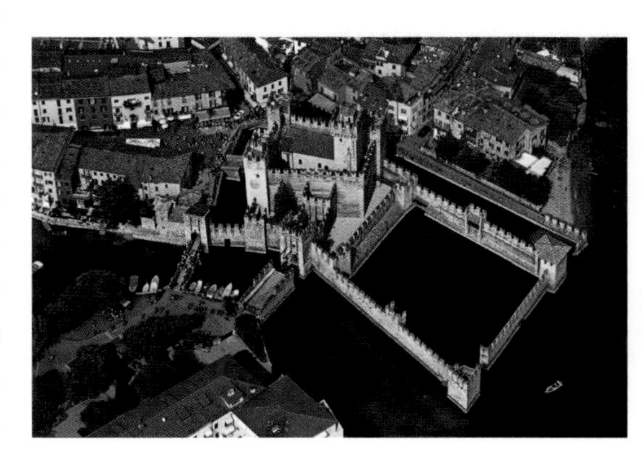

182-183 *The town of Griante is situated on "La Tremezzina," the western shore of Lake Como. In the background is the promontory of the Lavedo peninsula, at the tip of which is the Villa del Balbianello.*

183 *In 2002, the Villa del Balbianello was the spectacular set for* Star Wars II: Attack of the Clones, *directed by George Lucas. Four years later, some of the scenes from* Casino Royale *were filmed here.*

Lake Como: Three Branches, One Heart

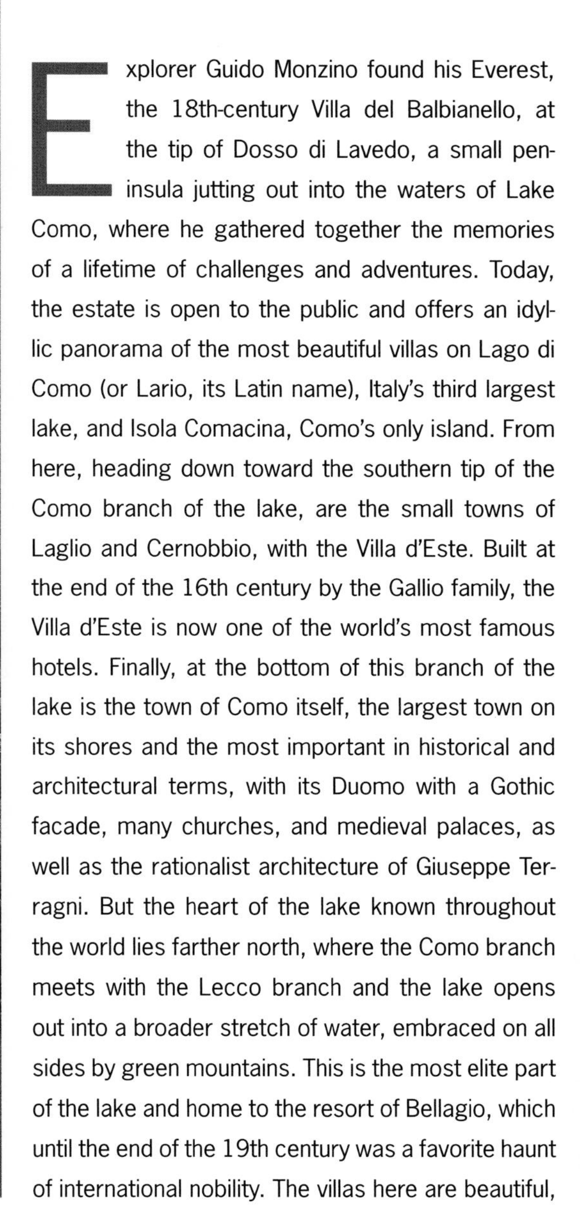

Explorer Guido Monzino found his Everest, the 18th-century Villa del Balbianello, at the tip of Dosso di Lavedo, a small peninsula jutting out into the waters of Lake Como, where he gathered together the memories of a lifetime of challenges and adventures. Today, the estate is open to the public and offers an idyllic panorama of the most beautiful villas on Lago di Como (or Lario, its Latin name), Italy's third largest lake, and Isola Comacina, Como's only island. From here, heading down toward the southern tip of the Como branch of the lake, are the small towns of Laglio and Cernobbio, with the Villa d'Este. Built at the end of the 16th century by the Gallio family, the Villa d'Este is now one of the world's most famous hotels. Finally, at the bottom of this branch of the lake is the town of Como itself, the largest town on its shores and the most important in historical and architectural terms, with its Duomo with a Gothic facade, many churches, and medieval palaces, as well as the rationalist architecture of Giuseppe Terragni. But the heart of the lake known throughout the world lies farther north, where the Como branch meets with the Lecco branch and the lake opens out into a broader stretch of water, embraced on all sides by green mountains. This is the most elite part of the lake and home to the resort of Bellagio, which until the end of the 19th century was a favorite haunt of international nobility. The villas here are beautiful, among them the Villas Melzi, Serbelloni, and Tremezzo, and the Villa Carlotta, with its botanical gardens well-known for their beautiful springtime azaleas. On the eastern shore, just north of where the lake divides, lies Varenna, with its colorful houses and the splendid Villa Monastero. Head south from Varenna to find "that branch of the Lake of Como, which turns toward the south..." made famous by novelist Alessandro Manzoni and characterized by the peaks of the Grigne and the Resegone mountains made of dolomite rock. Turn, instead, to the north and the Alto Lario, the upper and broader part of the lake, where the mountains rise ever higher, culminating at 8,556 feet (2608 meters) in Monte Legnone, on the eastern shore. At its base is one of the most beautiful monuments on the lake: the Cistercian Piona Abbey, founded in the 12th century on the Olgiasca peninsula, in the commune of Colico.

184-185 *Bellagio, at the junction of the two branches of Lake Como, is the quintessence of the beautiful towns and villages on the lake. The splendid Villa Melzi and the Villa Serbelloni are witnesses to the lake's long tradition of tourism.*

185 top *Built in 1568 as the summer residence for Cardinal Tolomeo Gallio, before becoming a hotel in 1873, Villa d'Este in Cernobbio belonged to Caroline of Brunswick, wife of George IV of England.*

185 bottom *Menaggio, on the western shore of Lake Como, the most famous of the towns on the central part of the lake, is popular among lovers of water sports for its marina and its charming lake front.*

The Borromeo Islands: An Invitation to the Palace

Isola Bella—the best known of the islands in the small archipelago on Lake Maggiore—is a hymn to love. Carlo III Borromeo named it in honor of his wife Isabella. And a love of beauty is everywhere in this treasure trove of wonders, 1,050 feet (320 meters) long and 590 feet (180 meters) wide, almost entirely occupied by the sumptuous baroque palace and its panoramic Italian gardens, conceived as a single and spectacular whole. Arriving from Stresa by ferry, the island looks like a large ship of marble, sailing the waters of Lake Maggiore, and changing color with the flowers as they bloom from March to September. The palace is worth visiting today more than ever, thanks to the reopening of the painting gallery, exhibiting 130 works from among the most important of the island's artistic heritage, with masterpieces from the Lombard baroque and copies made by great masters of the past. As well as the so-called Throne Room, there is a succession of furnished rooms, decorated with statues, paintings, and tapestries, and outside the palace artificial grottoes decorated with marine motifs. Equally impressive is the baroque garden, where ten sloping terraces rise into a pyramid, culminating in a statue of a unicorn, the heraldic symbol of the Borromeo family, being ridden by the figure of Love. A passion for plants and botany is the common thread binding Isola Bella with Isola Madre, the largest of the Borromeo Islands, where an orchard was transformed into a romantic English garden during the early 19th century. The flowers of the camellias, wisterias, azaleas, and the botanical gardens, where peacocks, parrots, and pheasants wander among plants originating in the furthest latitudes, attract many enthusiasts. The small 16th-century palace is also worth visiting, where you can journey back in time, thanks to the exquisite reconstruction of the period rooms, decorated with furnishings from the various historical estates of the Borromeo family.

186-187 *The baroque Palazzo Borromeo on Isola Bella has played host to many historical figures, including Napoleon Bonaparte, who stayed here in 1797, with his first wife Joséphine de Beauharnais.*

187 *Isola Superiore, also known as Isola dei Pescatori ("Fisherman's Island"), is the smallest of the Borromeo Islands and the only one to be inhabited throughout the year. The daily catch of fish can be enjoyed in many of the restaurants overlooking the lake.*

The Langhe: Rolling Hills and Rows of Vines

The first Italian "Academy of Taste" could only have been created in a place like the Langhe. Inaugurated in 2004, the University of Gastronomic Sciences is housed in the royal residence built by King Carlo Alberto of Savoy at Pollenzo, between Bra and Alba, in other words, between the cradle of Slow Food and the home of the white truffle. The union of art, architecture, and gastronomic excellence is a constant in the Langhe region. A tour in a hot air balloon—one of the many on offer locally—is the perfect way to gain a quick overview of the essential character of this part of southern Piedmont. Just see what surprises await you: a veritable sea of rolling hills where rows of vines are interspersed with castles and towers, clustered around timeless villages. Once back on terra firma, it is worthwhile exploring this fertile land, beginning perhaps in Alba, the city of a hundred towers, famous throughout the world for its truffles, which in November are the stars of the most famous (and expensive) food fair in Italy. But the Langhe is also synonymous with good wine, beginning with Barolo, "the wine of kings, the king of wines," which is produced in no fewer than 13 municipalities, including the village of Barolo itself. It is in fact Barolo's Castello dei Marchesi Falletti ("Castle of Marquis Falletti di Barolo") that houses the WiMu, the Wine Museum designed by François Confino, who also oversaw the preparations for the Museo del Cinema, housed in the Mole Antonelliana, and more recently, the Museo dell'Automobile, both of which are in Turin. For an unforgettable gastronomic experience, it is worth stopping at the Castello di Grinzane Cavour, the castle in the village of the same name, residence of the count of Cavour, Italy's first prime minister, from 1832. The count was responsible for the development of the vineyards in the area and for the birth of the great wines of the Langa ("Langhe" in old dialect), which today may be tasted at the Enoteca Regionale Piemontese, the wine store and restaurant housed in the castle's cellars. A few miles further south, it is the slender towers of the Castello di Serralunga ("Castle of Serralunga"), encircled by the village of Serralunga d'Alba, that captures the attention, which must be the most spectacular of the castles in the Langhe.

188 *Castello Falletti di Barolo is the only castle in the Langhe lies among the hills rather than being built on top of one. Italian writer Silvio Pellico worked in its library after being released from Špilberk Castle prison in Brno, Moravia.*

188-189 *From the ridge of the hill, the sleek lines of the Castello di Serralunga d'Alba dominate the landscape of the Langhe hills. It is one of the best-preserved 14th-century castles in the whole of Piedmont.*

190-191 *In the Langhe, time is counted in terms of vintages—those of its wines, from Barolo to Barbera and from Barbaresco to Dolcetto. The Lange hills are a very special destination for gastronomic tourism.*

192-193 *From Castello Brown, built around the year 1,000 on a promontory overlooking the entry to the harbor, Portofino looks beautiful, its famous square surrounded by colorful houses.*

Portofino's Piazzetta: Where Everybody Meets

A place with a name that has already become an international brand, synonymous with luxury and exclusivity; it would be impossible to contemplate any other fate for Portofino, a small fishing village in Liguria, whose first champion was none other than Guy de Maupassant. It was the French writer, in fact, who let the world know about this "hidden bay, with its olive trees and chestnut trees. A small village" that "spreads like a crescent moon around this quiet basin." Even today, people arriving for the first time at the small harbor hidden in the deep bay below the Portofino promontory are left quite speechless. Colorful houses huddle together around the small port, hugging the famous square in a tight embrace, offering a delightful welcome to those arriving by luxury yacht for an aperitif or to enjoy dinner in one of Portofino's jam-packed eateries. At the tiny tables of renowned restaurants like Puny and Pitosforo, international stars, industrialists, princes, and politicians rediscover, year after year, the pleasure of simplicity served in a dish of Ligurian-style sea bream or a plate of *pansotti* with walnut sauce. Behind the square, to the rear of the Aleppo pines and holm oaks, set in among the olive trees, hide the splendid villas of the visitors, both old and new, to the pearl of the Tigullio. But it is from the promontory that you'll find the most spectacular panorama. The church of San Giorgio ("St. George") can be reached on foot in just a few minutes, where the relics of the saint, which were brought to Italy from the Holy Land, are said to be held; to one side, there's a view of the sea, and to the other, a view of nearly all of Portofino. From here, it's possible to continue, passing villas and lush gardens, to the 15th-century Castello Brown, home of the British consul in Genoa, Montague Yeates Brown, from 1867. And it's no surprise to learn that this magical area inspired writer Elizabeth Von Arnim, a guest one spring of the fortunate British diplomat, to write her novel here, eloquently entitled *The Enchanted April*.

194-195 *The village of Vernazza—the pearl of the Cinque Terre—is dominated by the castrum, the medieval fortifications including a castle and round tower, and is characterized by its terraced hills of vineyards, olive groves, and lemon trees.*

195 *Riomaggiore, the most easterly and southerly of the Cinque Terre, owes much of its fame to the presence of the so-called Way of Love ("Via dell'Amore"), a cliff pathway overlooking the sea to the village of Manarola.*

The Cinque Terre: Where the Hills are Alive

The rebirth of Vernazza began with British architect Richard Rogers. Winner of the Pritzker Prize for architecture in 2007, he was responsible for the renovation of the historic center of the most characteristic of the villages of Cinque Terre, after it was buried in the mud following the tragic flood of 2011. Vernazza has already returned to normalcy, thanks primarily to the stubbornness of its inhabitants. People of great character, over the centuries the inhabitants of the Cinque Terre have succeeded in shaping the natural environment to their own advantage. Heroic, indeed, is the effort that goes into farming the *cian*, the local name for the terraces supported by dry stone walls, which run down the steep slopes into the Ligurian Sea. No one living in these enchanting villages along the 5 miles (8 kilometers) of rugged coastline, between Punta Mesco and Punta Montenero, has ever been afraid of hard work. Not even the tourists are fazed by the miles of pathways—not always easy to negotiate—that at one time represented the only means of access between Monterosso, Vernazza, Corniglia, Manarola, and Riomaggiore, the five villages inscribed for their cultural landscape by UNESCO in the list of World Heritage Sites in 1997. The houses, as well, contribute to the romance of the Cinque Terre: highly colorful at Riomaggiore, the oldest village, and at Vernazza, whose tiny harbor has as a backdrop the castle tower and the church of Santa Maria di Antiochia, a masterpiece of Ligurian Romanesque architecture. At Manarola, the houses cluster around its very narrow harbor clamped between two rocky outcrops, while Corniglia, the most "rural" of the Cinque Terre's five villages, is perched, as if by magic, on a cliff overlooking the sea, reached by a flight of 377 steps. Lastly, more open and less hemmed in by cliffs, and with more amenities, is Monterosso, divided into two distinct parts: Fegina, renowned for its beach (a real rarity in this area), and the old town, with its narrow alleyways and colorful buildings contrasting pleasantly with the two-tone facade of the 13th-century church of San Giovanni Battista.

The Ancient Skyscrapers of San Gimignano

Why do people compete to build every higher skyscrapers? Is it simply a demonstration of supremacy? In San Gimignano, this idea is ancient or, to be more exact, medieval history. In the 1300s the power of a family in Val d'Elsa was measured in terms of height. The wealthiest families built over 70 towers in the city, creating a skyline that has often been compared with that of Manhattan. Only 14 towers remain today, but to get an idea of how this place must have looked to the pilgrims who stopped here on their way along the Via Francigena, you only need to see the reconstruction of the town at the height of its glory, on a scale of 1:100, in the new San Gimignano 1300 museum. There is certainly no shortage of historical evidence, as you will realize by simply walking across Piazza Duomo and Piazza della Cisterna, the city's two symbolic squares. Piazza Duomo is dominated by the magnificent Collegiate Church of Santa Maria Assunta, designed in the Tuscan Romanesque style and housing frescoes from the Sienese school and wooden statues by Jacopo della Quercia. To the left of the cathedral is the Palazzo Comunale, home to the important civic museum and flanked by the Torre Grossa, the highest tower in the city, at 77 feet (54 meters). The effort involved in climbing to the top is more than repaid by the magnificent panoramic view over San Gimignano and the valley beyond. The city's oldest tower, the Torre del Podestà, also known as the Torre della Rognosa ("tower of troubles"—it was formerly a prison) soars over the square along with the Torri Gemelle dei Salvucci, the twin towers that belonged to the most important Guelph family, the Salvucci. On the opposite side stand the Torri Gemelle degli Ardinghelli, which belonged to the Ardinghelli family, their eternal Ghibelline rivals. A passageway connects the square to the Piazza della Cisterna, dominated at the center by an octagonal well, in the shadow of the Torre dei Becci, the Torre dei Cugnanesi, Palazzo Razzi, and the Torre del Diavolo. From here, after getting pleasantly lost in a maze of back streets, you reach the Church of St. Augustine, behind whose austere facade are some exquisite works of art, the highlight of which is a cycle of frescoes by Benozzo Gozzoli and the majolica tile floor by Andrea della Robbia.

196-197 In the 14th century, the Sienese countryside around the village of San Gimignano became highly profitable thanks to the trade in wool, the white wine grape Vernaccia, and saffron, which was mainly used for dyeing.

198-199 *The clay-rich soil in the area southeast of Siena gives rise to a unique landscape, where rolling hills crossed by rows of cypresses and dotted with isolated farms alternate with calanchi and biancane.*

199 *Just outside the medieval center of the town of Asciano, in the heart of the Crete Senesi, is the extraordinary Desserto di Accona ("Accona Desert"), with its characteristic lunar appearance resulting from the soil composed of clay and rock salt.*

200-201 *The Abbey of Monte Oliveto Maggiore is situated on top of a hill covered with cypress trees. The Olivetan monks not only stimulated agriculture in the Crete Senesi, but also developed the artistic technique of wood inlay.*

Crete Senesi and its Lunar Landscape

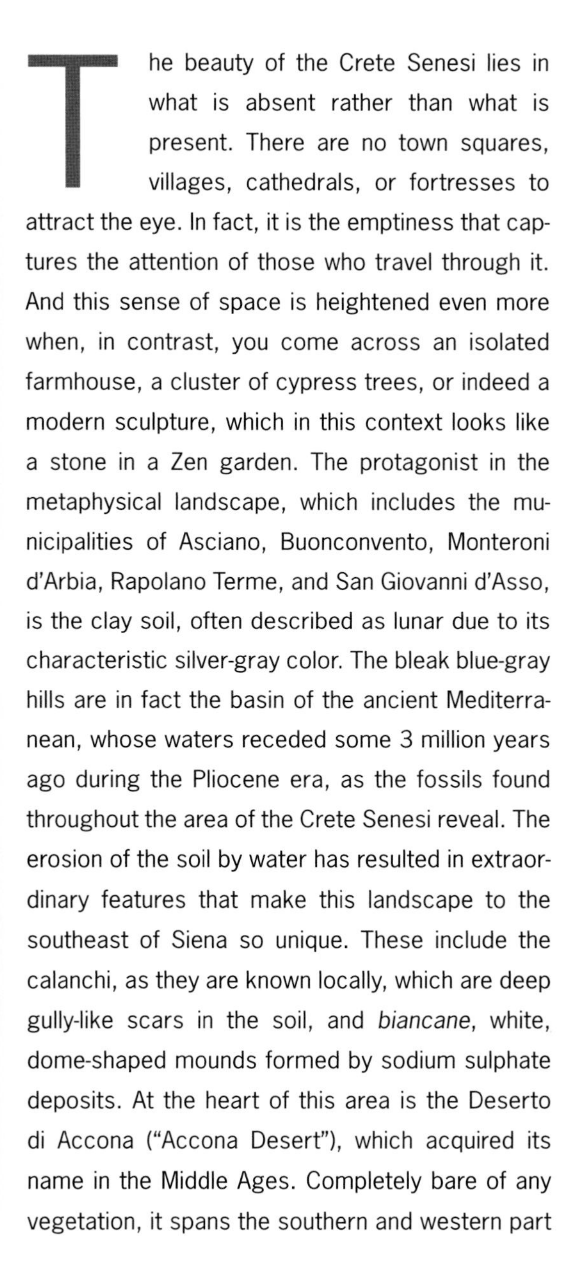

The beauty of the Crete Senesi lies in what is absent rather than what is present. There are no town squares, villages, cathedrals, or fortresses to attract the eye. In fact, it is the emptiness that captures the attention of those who travel through it. And this sense of space is heightened even more when, in contrast, you come across an isolated farmhouse, a cluster of cypress trees, or indeed a modern sculpture, which in this context looks like a stone in a Zen garden. The protagonist in the metaphysical landscape, which includes the municipalities of Asciano, Buonconvento, Monteroni d'Arbia, Rapolano Terme, and San Giovanni d'Asso, is the clay soil, often described as lunar due to its characteristic silver-gray color. The bleak blue-gray hills are in fact the basin of the ancient Mediterranean, whose waters receded some 3 million years ago during the Pliocene era, as the fossils found throughout the area of the Crete Senesi reveal. The erosion of the soil by water has resulted in extraordinary features that make this landscape to the southeast of Siena so unique. These include the calanchi, as they are known locally, which are deep gully-like scars in the soil, and *biancane*, white, dome-shaped mounds formed by sodium sulphate deposits. At the heart of this area is the Deserto di Accona ("Accona Desert"), which acquired its name in the Middle Ages. Completely bare of any vegetation, it spans the southern and western part of the territory of Asciano, a charming medieval village and commune north of the Abbey of Monte Oliveto Maggiore. The rough landscape of the Crete Senesi seems to enhance the spirituality of the monastery, founded in 1313 by the Sienese noble Giovanni Tolomei, who renounced his wealth to live as a hermit in a community inspired by the Benedictine rule. The abbey welcomes visitors with an avenue lined by tall stately cypresses leading to the Gothic church, with its exquisite 16th-century carved wooden choir. The Great Cloister houses important examples of Italian Renaissance art: scenes depicting the Life of St. Benedict by Luca Signorelli and Sodoma from the late 15th and early 16th centuries. The library within the complex is also of enormous value, containing over 40,000 volumes, many of which have passed through the hands of those Benedictines who were responsible for the monastery's renowned Institute of Book Restoration.

Val d'Orcia: Where Man and Nature are in Harmony

The perfect setting for the perfect town: for Enea Silvio Piccolomini, who became Pope Pius II, it was only in Val d'Orcia that his dream could be realized. His goal was to transform a small medieval village into an urban Utopia, an ideal place where people could live in harmony together and with nature. And so Pienza was born, a Renaissance jewel in the region that extends between the Crete Senesi and the slopes of Monte Amiata, a natural landscape shaped by man in his constant pursuit of beauty but tempered by a respect for nature. The landscape that the traveler crosses is gentle, along ancient roads that have marked the region profoundly, such as the Roman Via Cassia and Via Francigena, the pilgrimage route from northern Europe to Rome. Cresting one hill of clay after another, the vegetation alternates between vines and Mediterranean macchia (shrubland), and olive groves and rows of cypresses; it is a sea of green and yellow, lapping at the slopes of Monte Amiata, which are covered by a forest of beach and chestnut trees. In Val d'Orcia, the marriage between art and landscape reaches perfection, as UNESCO has recognized, having inscribed the region as a World Heritage Site in 2004. Villages blend in harmoniously with the landscape, including, in particular, Montalcino, surrounded by woods and vineyards that produce not just the extraordinary Brunello red wine but also honey, and San Quirico d'Orcia, with its beautiful collegiate church and the Horti Leonini, a superb example of a 16th-century Italian garden. Not far away, Bagno Vignoni is one of the most arresting and best preserved medieval villages in Tuscany, situated around a large reservoir holding thermal water of volcanic origin at a temperature of 125.6°F (52°C). Just as magical, in Monte Amiata, are the hot springs of Bagni San Filippo, where white limestone deposits have transformed the landscape, and the thermal water spills down through small waterfalls into a series of shallow basins, right in the middle of the forest. Nearby, at Radicofani, it is the work of man that stands out this time, its imposing fortress having dominated Val d'Orcia, Monte Amiata, and Monte Cetona for 1,000 years.

202 On the hills of Val d'Orcia, isolated farms are surrounded by oak forests, olive groves, and vineyards, whose grapes produce great wines like the celebrated Brunello di Montalcino and the Vino Nobile di Montepulciano.

202-203 In 1459 the humanist Pope Pius II developed the project to transform the village of Corsignano into the ideal town of Pienza, inspired by the new values and models of the Florentine Quattrocento.

204-205 The town of Spoleto, rich in ancient Roman remains, has preserved its medieval appearance intact, dating back to when it was first a Lombard duchy, then later a center of the Papal States.

205 The Cathedral of Santa Maria Assunta was built in 1067 upon the remains of a 9th-century church. The Romanesque-style facade is decorated with a large mosaic of the Benedictory Christ and five rose windows.

The Curtain Rises on Spoleto

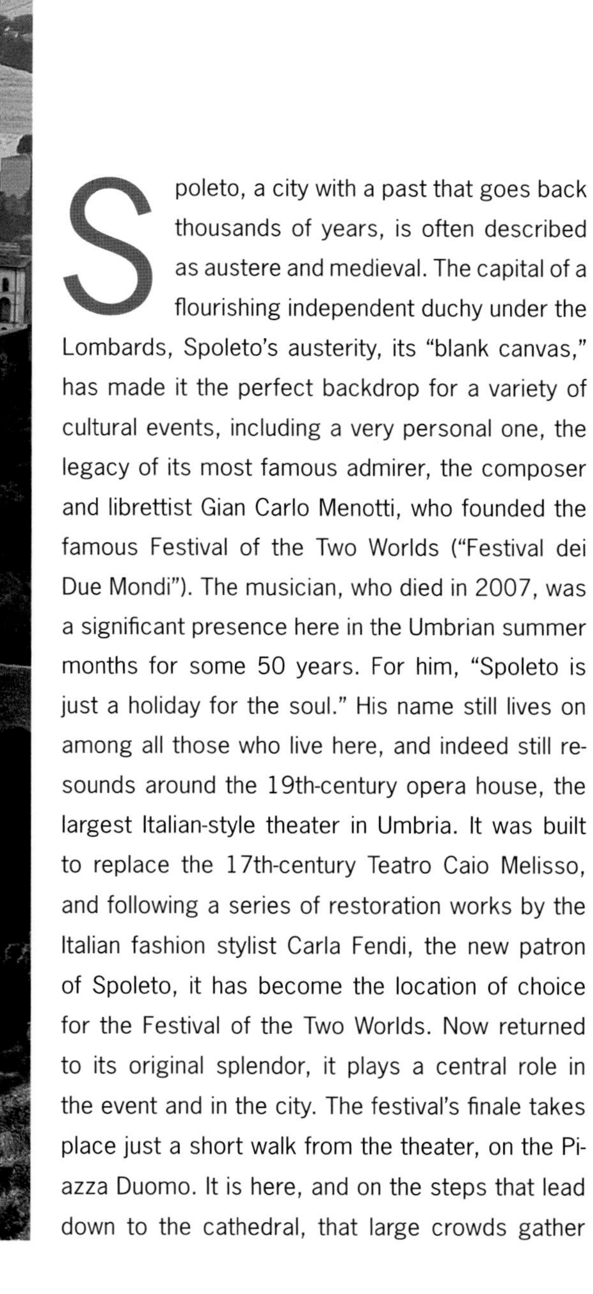

Spoleto, a city with a past that goes back thousands of years, is often described as austere and medieval. The capital of a flourishing independent duchy under the Lombards, Spoleto's austerity, its "blank canvas," has made it the perfect backdrop for a variety of cultural events, including a very personal one, the legacy of its most famous admirer, the composer and librettist Gian Carlo Menotti, who founded the famous Festival of the Two Worlds ("Festival dei Due Mondi"). The musician, who died in 2007, was a significant presence here in the Umbrian summer months for some 50 years. For him, "Spoleto is just a holiday for the soul." His name still lives on among all those who live here, and indeed still resounds around the 19th-century opera house, the largest Italian-style theater in Umbria. It was built to replace the 17th-century Teatro Caio Melisso, and following a series of restoration works by the Italian fashion stylist Carla Fendi, the new patron of Spoleto, it has become the location of choice for the Festival of the Two Worlds. Now returned to its original splendor, it plays a central role in the event and in the city. The festival's finale takes place just a short walk from the theater, on the Piazza Duomo. It is here, and on the steps that lead down to the cathedral, that large crowds gather to enjoy the last concert, a magical performance with the spectacular backdrop of the Romanesque facade of Spoleto cathedral, dedicated to the Assumption of the Blessed Virgin Mary, with its five rose windows and Byzantine-style mosaic. In the interior, the apse is decorated with frescoes that depict scenes from the life of the Virgin ("*Storie della Vergine*") by Filippino Lippi, whose tomb is in the cathedral. The festival also celebrates the world of ancient Rome; the Roman Theater, restored in 1954, hosts ballets and concerts, a rather more edifying use for the building than during the Middle Ages, when it was exploited as a stone quarry for the construction of Rocca Albornoziana, the fortress on top of St. Elias Hill. This is the highest point in Spoleto and offers a spectacular view over the entire valley.

Ponza and the Pontine Islands

They couldn't be more different. And yet, together, they make a perfect pair, the ideal vacation destination. If the small, relatively flat island of Ventotene sounds a lone, quiet voice, a place inviting contemplation, Ponza is full-blooded and frivolous, perfect for those who prefer not to renounce worldly pleasures, even if it means having to enjoy an aperitif on the square in the company of a small crowd of people. They could not be any more different in color. From a distance, Ponza looks like a brilliant white crescent, its village encircling the harbor, buildings scrambling upward like the terraces of an amphitheater, while Ventotene, hewn out of the tuff, appears yellow, with a few touches of bright red. For centuries both islands shared the same fate as places of exile. Ponza played host to Agrippina the Younger as well as Pope Silverius, who later became the island's patron saint and is celebrated on June 20 with one of the busiest and most moving processions in the Mediterranean. Ventotene welcomed Agrippina the Elder's mother Julia the Elder, who was confined by her father Augustus in the great villa that extended over some 985 feet (300 meters) in length and 330 feet (100 meters) in width on the promontory of Punta Eolo, where its ruins can still be seen today. Also held on Ventotene, during the Fascist era, were Italian politicians, partisans, and intellectuals, from the former president of the Italian Republic, Sandro Pertini, to the founding father of Europe, Altiero Spinelli. The latter two were "guests" in the prison built by the Bourbons on the nearby island of Santo Stefano, an Italian penal colony designed by Francesco Carpi, a pupil of Vanvitelli. Those "exiled" on the islands today have a much more enjoyable stay. A boat is indispensable, especially for reaching the smaller islands: Palmarola, 6 miles (10 kilometers) west of Ponza, has natural amphitheaters, cliffs, grottoes, and rock columns that look as though they were carved by an artist; and Zannone, the most northerly island in the Pontine Archipelago, is covered with holm oaks and Mediterranean *macchia* (shrubland), and inhabited by nothing more than a colony of wild sheep.

206 Built by the Bourbons, and dating back to the second half of the 18th century, the port of Ponza is the entrance to the island, the largest in the archipelago. The town grew up around the semicircular harbor.

206-207 The highest part of the island of Ponza—5 miles (8 kilometers) long and 5,906 feet (1,800 meters) at its widest point—is Monte Guardia, 919 feet (280 meters) above sea level. On its summit is a naval signal light no longer in use.

208-209 The inhabited section of Ventotene, on the eastern side of the island, forms the backdrop to the Roman port. The Bourbon village of Ventotene developed around the castle and the Church of Santa Candida, the patron saint of the island.

The Crystal-Clear Waters of the Maddalena Archipelago

Small, but feisty! Behind the Maddalena Archipelago is a long history of struggle that has ensured it remains the natural wonder that it is today: 19 square miles (50 square kilometers) in area, with 112 miles (180 kilometers) of coastline, among the most beautiful in the world. Even Napoleon was forced to give in to the warlike spirit of the islanders of La Maddalena, who, led by Italian patriot Domenico Millelire, succeeded in resisting him. The islands have also shown themselves capable of holding their own in the face of human folly and the threat of over development that have hung over them for years. With the establishment of the Parco Nazionale dell'Arcipelago della Maddalena ("La Maddalena Archipelago National Park") and, more recently, a green alliance with neighboring Corsica, the seven principal islands and their little sisters have now been preserved, recognized universally as one of the most beautiful areas in the Mediterranean. In fact, everything now focuses on the natural heritage of the islands, from the departure of the U.S. Navy's armed forces (and their dollars), to the G8 summit that was going to be held here in 2009, but was moved at the last minute to Aquila, in central Italy. This missed opportunity must have led to some reflection, and now, in the beautiful islands of the Gallura region, off the northeastern coast of Sardinia, the focus is on a new model of development related to tourism and the environment. On the main island of La Maddelena, where 18th-century buildings line the port of Cala Gavetta, dominated by the stronghold of the Guardia Vecchia ("the old guard"), there are striking views to be discovered along the scenic road above the Cala Spalmatore. All along its 12-mile (20 kilometer) stretch, there are views of the Sardinian coastline, Corsica, and the other islands of the archipelago. One of these, Caprera, can be reached by crossing the Passo della Moneta (the "coin pass"), a bridge-dam that leads to the island where the "Hero of the Two Worlds," Giuseppe Garibaldi, spent his last 20 years fighting an uphill battle to transform the island's granite rocks into fields suitable for cultivating. Returning to the sea, history gives way to a dreamlike natural environment, like that on Budelli, the island with pink sand, immortalized in a scene from Michelangelo Antonioni's film *Red Desert*, or on Spargi, covered entirely with Mediterranean macchia (shrubland), and boasting splendid beaches at its eastern end, such as Cala Corsara and Cala Granara, surrounded by statue-like rocks of granite.

210 *Pink beach on Budelli. The Parco Nazionale dell'Arcipelago della Maddalena ("La Maddalena Archipelago National Park"), established in 1994, protects 69 square miles (18,000 hectares) 20 square miles (5,134 hectares) of land, 50 square miles (13,000 hectares) of marine sea, and 112 miles (180 kilometers) of coastline.*

211 *The beach that opens along the southern part of the island of Budelli owes its particular coloring to the tiny fragments of* Miniacina miniacea, *a microorganism that flourishes on the local seagrass.*

The Vertiginous Beauty of the Amalfi Coast

"There is only one narrow street and it does not come down to the water. Everything else is stairs, some of them as steep as ladders. You do not walk to visit a friend, you either climb or slide." So wrote John Steinbeck about Positano for *Harper's Bazaar*: a chronicle of the author's journey that could well apply to the entire Amalfi Coast, a fine southern beauty, but not an easy conquest. It is the combination of mountain and sea that has apparently rendered the landscape so inaccessible and so intriguing, sculpting a universe of fjords, promontories, natural arches, coves, and inlets that are now emblematic of Mediterranean beauty. The character of this particular stretch of Campanian coast between Positano and Vietri sul Mare is mirrored by those who came here and fell in love with it, passionate personalities like Richard Wagner and his wife Cosima; Wagner was so charmed by the Villa Rufolo at Ravello that it was here that the German composer conceived Klingsor's magic garden for his *Parsifal*. In the village perched on a rocky bluff of the Monti Lattari, the mountains forming the most enchanting natural balcony over the towns of Amalfi and Minori, the divine Hollywood actress Greta Garbo and conductor Leopold Stokowski dallied in romance, and Gore Vidal, the most caustic of American writers, had a villa. The fiery temperaments of Italian actress Anna Magnani and director Roberto Rossellini, found asylum in "the world's most beautiful gorge," the Furore fjord, with its settlement scattered across the mountainside overlooking the sea. Clinging to a spur of the Monti Lattari, with its exhausting climbs and bougainvilleas ablaze between clusters of white houses, it is Positano that has, above all, fascinated painters and musicians. Perhaps it was the mythical sirens, said to have lived on the Li Galli islands, who drew so many artists here; these three small islands off the coast of Positano were once owned by the great dancer Rudolf Nureyev. Visitors to Amalfi can explore its cathedral, dedicated to the Apostle St. Andrew, with a spectacular neo-Gothic facade and Romanesque bell tower, as well as the Valle dei Mulini ("Valley of the Mills"), the old industrial zone dating back to the time when Amalfi and its region was a maritime republic, where the renowned Amalfi paper is produced.

212 Amalfi Cathedral was created from two adjacent and communicating basilicas, the Church of Santa Maria Assunta and the Church of Sant'Andrea Apostolo. The current facade dates from 1891 and is decorated with Byzantine-style mosaics.

212-213 With its settlements scattered partway across the lower stretches of the slopes of Monte Tre Pizzi (3,681 feet/1,122 meters), Praiano was the summer residence for the doges of Amalfi during the heyday of the Republic of Amalfi.

214 TOP THE PANORAMA THAT CAN BE ADMIRED FROM THE TERRACED GARDENS OF VILLA RUFOLO AT RAVELLO IS ONE OF THE FINEST ALONG THE AMALFI COAST. THE PARK OWES ITS PRESENT APPEARANCE TO SCOTTISH PHILANTHROPIST, ART COLLECTOR, AND BOTANIST, SIR FRANCIS NEVILLE REID.

214 BOTTOM BUILT ON THE SLOPES OF MONTE COMUNE AND MONTE SANT'ANGELO A TRE PIZZI, THE ELEGANT VILLAGE OF POSITANO IS UNMISTAKABLE WITH ITS CUBE-SHAPED, LIME-WASHED HOUSES, AND SPHERICAL ROOFS.

214-215 ALLEYS, ARCHES, COURTYARDS, AND STAIRWAYS EMBROIDER THE PICTURESQUE VILLAGE OF ATRANI, ONE OF THE BEST PRESERVED ALONG THE COAST. THE NOBLEST FAMILIES OF AMALFI LIVED HERE DURING THE HEYDAY OF THE MARITIME REPUBLICS.

Capri: The Perfect Balance of Nature and Culture

The charm of Capri is a lot like the irresistible attraction of its famous raviolis—both are simple, but at the same time, amazing, the result of a perfect balance of ingredients. If *caciotta*, Parmigiano-Reggiano, and marjoram in the right proportions have been pleasing the most discerning palates for years, so also has the combination of natural beauty, art, culture, worldliness, and tradition that makes this small island in the Gulf of Naples unique. It would be difficult to find another place, where, in just a few moments, you can move from somewhere bursting at the seams with people—like the famous square La Piazzetta in the summer—to the silence of a pathway high on a clifftop over the sea. To find the best of Capri, you have to go on foot: climb the road leading up to Villa Jovis, the most beautiful of the 12 villas built on the island by Emperor Tiberius, or take the striking (and demanding) Pizzolungo promenade, which winds its way through the Mediterranean vegetation part way up the coastal slope, to reach a masterpiece of rationalist architecture. The Villa Malaparte, clinging to the top of the Massullo promontory, has a sublime view of the famous Faraglioni, three tall stacks of rock rising out of the sea nearby. Also looking out over the Faraglioni is the famous and symbolic Via Krupp, a fabulous scenic path that was reopened in 2008 after 32 years of restoration work. It comprises nearly 2 miles (3 kilometers) of switchbacks carved out of the rock above the sea in 1902, on the orders of German steel magnate Friedrich Alfred Krupp. The road that winds between the Gardens of Augustus and the port of Marina Piccola is just one of the many testimonies of the whole world's love for Capri, such as the villa built in the late 1800s by Swedish psychiatrist Axel Munthe in the quiet village of Anacapri. His Villa San Michele, built on the ruins of an ancient chapel, is the most frequently visited site on the island after the celebrated Blue Grotto. In the garden and among the rooms, where writers Rainer Maria Rilke and Oscar Wilde, and actress Greta Garbo stayed as guests, you can admire the rich collection of antiquities assembled by Munthe over the 50 or so years that he lived on the island.

216 From Marina Grande, the main port, the cable car takes you directly to the heart of the island and Piazza Umberto I, the square known throughout the world as "La Piazzetta," set against a backdrop of the domes of the former Cathedral of Santo Stefano.

216-217 Symbols of Capri, the Faraglioni rise to 328 feet (100 meters) above the surface of the sea, just off the southeastern coast of the island. The outer stack, called Scopolo, is the only place in the world where the blue lizard can be found.

218-219 Perched on a hill overlooking the sea, the white city of Ostuni is dominated by its cathedral, with its late Gothic facade, and by the majolica-tiled dome of the Church of San Vito Martire (called "delle Monacelle").

219 The pinnacles on top of the whitewashed limestone trulli. The various shapes (disks, spheres, cones, pyramids) are said to be linked with the cult of the sun practiced by ancient peoples.

220-221 The "balcony" looking out over the Murge plateau, the Mother Church of San Giorgio dominates the center of the town of Locorotondo, named for its circular layout.

In the Sun-Drenched Itria Valley

The race to see the *trulli* of Apulia began in the late 1980s, and since then there has been no let up. Today more than ever, the mysterious conical huts are the "white gold" of the Itria Valley, a broad and undulating karst basin on the southeastern Murge plateau. In this region, which includes the towns of Locorotondo, Martina Franca, Alberobello, Cisternino, and Ceglie Messapica, even the farms and the lamie—the typical farmhouses with vaulted roofs—attract the famous and non-famous alike, in search of a reassuring return to basics. It's difficult to resist the dazzling charm of Ostuni: with its whitewashed walls, it looks like a Greek island that has been transported magically to an Italian hilltop. To reinforce the feeling of displacement, the sea appears remarkably close when viewed from the top of the village, beside the 15th-century cathedral and the polychrome dome of the former Convento delle Monacelle. Balconies with panoramic views are ubiquitous in the Itria Valley, including in Locorotondo, the most spectacular of the valley's towns and villages, from where there are views of dry stone walls, olive trees, and vines as far as the eye can see, dotted here and there with the conical shapes of the *trulli*. It is here, in the shade of the *cummerse*, the pointed gable roofs typical of the area, that the grapes are gathered for making the famous Locorotondo DOC white wine. Red wine, however, goes better with a lunch in the *fornelli* (literally, "stovetop burners"), the characteristic butcher shops with kitchens that are very popular, especially in Cisternino, a small town of winding alleys, courtyards, outside staircases, balconies with flowers, and archways, where the sudden transition from light to shade recalls a North African casbah. But to see the most amazing examples of the region's special architecture, we need to go to Alberobello, the "trulli capital." Thanks to its large concentration of these buildings—as many as 1,500 were constructed, some dating back to AD 500 in the districts of Aia Piccola and Monti—Alberobello won recognition in 1996 as a UNESCO World Heritage Site.

Matera: Ancient City of Living Rock

A record-breaking event was held here at Christmas 2010, when Matera entered the *Guinness Book of World Records* for staging the largest number of living figures in a nativity scene at Sasso Caveoso. But in this city in what was the ancient region of Lucania, the lights of a record-breaking nativity scene are lit 365 days a year, when the Sassi are transformed into a firmament of rock. The Sassi, or "stones," comprise two districts of ancient dwellings hewn out of the deep karst ravine called La Gravina, separated from one another by the rocky spur of the Civita. It is at night that this unique urban landscape, dug out of the calcarenite stone, and inhabited continuously since the Paleolithic era, comes to life, having seduced first Pier Paolo Pasolini, who filmed *The Gospel According to St. Matthew* here in 1964, and then Mel Gibson, 40 years later, for his *The Passion of the Christ.* Matera is an architectural masterpiece, and with its reservoirs excavated out of the calcarenite stone, it remains one of the oldest examples of environmental sustainability in the world. Strong legs are needed to explore Sasso Barisano and Sasso Caveoso, and to negotiate the stairways, alleys, and caves between the constructed and excavated cities, where the ruggedness and extreme gradient of the terrain have not deterred the architects of this extraordinary town, which in 1993 was inscribed in UNESCO's World Heritage list. The rock-hewn churches, dating as far back as the 7th century AD, are the most precious "stones" of the Sassi; to date, 155 of these have been counted, inside and outside Matera, often decorated with beautiful frescoes, like the complex of Santa Lucia alle Malve, the church of Santa Maria de Idris, and the church of San Giovanni. Since 1978, the Church of the Madonna delle Virtù and the Church of San Nicola dei Greci above it, have been exhibiting work by the most important names in international sculpture. Contemporary sculpture is also celebrated in MUSMA, the museum where, amid the baroque architecture and the tombs of Palazzo Pomarici, modern sculpture adds its final tribute to the ancient carved city.

222 At sunset the inhabited part of Sasso Barisano is even more atmospheric. With buildings piled up against each other and tufaceous rocky walls riddled with caves, the town is absolutely unique.

222-223 Matera Cathedral was constructed in the Apulian-Romanesque style on the Colle della Civita, where the two settlements of Sasso Barisano and Sasso Caveoso meet, forming this Lucanian city's complex historical center.

224-225 *The Old Town of Gallipoli, connected to the mainland by a bridge, is the historic center of the Salento peninsula, which enjoyed a period of great prosperity in the 17th century thanks to the activity of its port.*

Gallipoli: On the Waterfront

Perched at the edge of the Ionian Sea, Gallipoli almost looks as though it's about to sail away, just like the ships that, since the 17th century, have been setting sail from its port each day, transporting over 26,400 gallons (100,000 liters) of oil all over the world. The historic center of what is known as the Pearl of Salento is located on an island, which is connected to the mainland and the new town that developed in the 19th century, by a bridge and seven arches constructed in the 17th century. The winding alleyways, courtyards, and white, lime-washed houses of the historic center are reminiscent of a city of the Orient, even if the baroque terraces and old buildings, many built in the fine stone of nearby Lecce, soon reveal that you are in fact in Salento, in the southeastern Apulia. In the center of the upper part of the old town is the Cathedral of St. Agatha, the greatest example of the local baroque style, which was constructed upon a small medieval church dedicated to St. John Chrysostom. The interior of the building, based on the Latin-cross plan, is frequently referred to as an authentic "picture gallery" owing to its wealth of paintings by 17th- and 18th-century artists from Naples and the Salento peninsula. Standing guard for the old town and the port is the Castello Angioino, surrounded almost entirely by the sea and a veritable encyclopedia in stone of the history of Gallipoli. The castle was rebuilt in the 17th century by Giorgio Martini of Siena, a major expert on military architecture of the time, incorporating the previous fortress, of Angevin origins, which, in turn, was built upon a Byzantine fortification. Square in plan, the castello has four great towers, to which the so-called Ravelin was added in the 16th century, a round tower forming a sort of outer bastion. From here, crossing over the 17th-century bridge just behind the harbor, you arrive at one of the most renowned and discussed monuments in Gallipoli, the Greek Fountain, at one time believed to be Hellenistic in origin, but in all probability the work of an able sculptor from the 16th century.

226-227 *From Vulcano's Gran Cratere, you can see over to Vulcanello and Lipari. The closest to the coast of Sicily, Vulcano was created from the fusion of several volcanoes, the largest of which is the Fossa cone.*

The Aeolian Islands: An Arc of Volcanic Beauty

The Aeolian Islands, the "seven sisters" off the northern coast of Sicily, all of volcanic origin, have the very wind in their name. According to myth, it was on Lipari, the principal island, that the god Aeolus lived, who tamed and controlled the winds. During the summer, those same winds swell the sails of the boats that make their way between the islands. Approaching by water is the best way to discover their different characters, beginning with Vulcano, closest to Sicily and known for its distinctly cantankerous nature. According to myth, this black island, created by the fusing of four volcanoes, is where Hephaestus had his forge. The largest, the Fossa cone, culminates in the Gran Cratere at a height of 1,283 feet (391 meters), a crater suffused by sulfurous vapors that stain the stone yellow and create a landscape of disquieting beauty. Equally impressive is the spectacular view that rewards those who make the climb up to the top of Stromboli to admire the sunset at 3,012 feet (918 meters). One of the world's most active volcanoes, when it erupts in a show of spectacular fireworks, ash rains down onto the glowing Sciara del Fuoco ("Stream of Fire"), the trail of lava that pours into the sea. Much milder in character, Salina is the second largest island after Lipari, and the greenest of the archipelago; capers are grown here, along with the prized grapes used to produce an excellent Malvasia wine. Panarea, the smallest and most exclusive of all the islands, has abandoned agriculture in favor of tourism, though without sacrificing its beauty. Its white houses with blue doors recall those in villages on the Cyclades. Less tame is the beauty of the more remote islands, Filicudi and the rather more austere Alicudi, where mule tracks are the paths leading up its steep flanks. By comparison, the main island Lipari seems like a real metropolis, with an historic center dominated by a fortress on a promontory, whose massive walls were built by the Spanish under Holy Roman Emperor Charles V. There are many surprises in store in the island's diminutive principal town, perched at the edge of the sea, including the Aeolian Archaeological Museum, situated on the castle's acropolis, a small gem telling the story of half a century of excavations and findings in the archipelago.

228 TOP *Pollara is one of the most picturesque corners of Salina, the most fertile island in the Aeolians. The village lies at the center of a half crater. The other half has sunk into the sea, leaving just a rocky stack.*

228 BOTTOM *Stromboli is the most active volcano in Europe, and one of the world's five volcanoes with permanent eruptive activity. The island's inhabitants call it Iddu (meaning "Him" in Sicilian), as though to highlight its divine nature.*

228-229 *Between the two inlets of Marina Lunga and Marina Corta, the Lipari's stronghold, known as "Il Castello," rises high above the sea. Behind the Spanish-built walls, the remains of the Norman cathedral can be seen.*

Etna: The Mountain of Fire

You could describe the landscape around the craters at the summit of Mount Etna as lunar—or even Martian. It is no coincidence that the robots designed by Alenia and the European Space Agency for the Mars mission were tested here, on the slopes of the highest active volcano in Europe, at the lava fields of Piano delle Concazze (9,186 feet/2,800 meters). Above 8,200 feet (2,500 meters), the mountain landscape feels truly supernatural, but Nature herself prepares hikers for the extremes of desert, lava, and fire by gradually pruning back all of her abundance. The belt of citrus orchards and prickly pears on the lower slopes is the first to go, replaced by olive trees and vineyards, with groves of almond trees on the western side and hazelnuts on the northeastern side. Then oak and chestnut woods give way to beech trees, until eventually the only vegetation left is a few tenacious *Rumex* bushes, flowery cushions of *Anthemis*, and *Saponaria* plants. Then comes the desert, a physical manifestation of the indomitable nature of this volcano, with its four active craters at the summit and about 300 eruptive vents: a gigantic boiler that must eject over 4,000 tons of gas and sulfur dioxide each day in order to release the build-up of internal pressure. First erupting 500,000 years ago, the volcano is in continual evolution and even its height (currently around 10,800 feet/3,300 meters) varies year on year, depending on volcanic activity; the biggest eruptions can be enormously destructive, like those of 1381 and 1669, and threaten the nearby villages, even on the lower slopes. The eruptions of adventive cones on the sides of the volcano are especially feared, like that of Montagnola, on the upper southern slope. The eastern slope is almost entirely occupied by the Valle del Bove, a gigantic volcanic depression 3.7 miles wide and 4.3 miles long (6 x 7 kilometers), where most of the lava flows from Etna come together. The origin of this impressive chasm—the edge of which is a favorite destination for excursions to Mount Etna—is attributed to the collapse of the Trifoglietti, the two ancient eruptive cones on which the present volcano is built.

230 The river of lava, known locally as "La Sciara," glows in the night. It flows down the sides of the volcano and over remarkable distances before solidifying. Many of these lava rivers culminate in the Valle del Bove.

230-231 A column of smoke emerges from the main crater of Etna, the highest volcano in Europe at 10,827 feet (3,300 meters). The Parco dell'Etna ("Etna Park") was established in 1987 to protect the area's natural heritage.

Archaeology: The Roots of History

"Whatever one does, one always rebuilds the monument in one's own way. But it is already something gained to have used only the original stones," wrote Marguerite Yourcenar in the Notebooks in the epigraph to her book Memoirs of Hadrian. *And it is precisely these "original stones" that have inspired and nurtured Italian art and architecture. The Italian peninsula has been able to develop artistically due to a sensitive awareness of its own past and an incredible archaeological heritage, a key point of reference for the arts throughout the ages.*

Andrea Palladio and the Italian and European neoclassical architects took inspiration from the Pantheon, defined by Stendhal as representing "the most beautiful memories of Roman antiquity." On the orders of Barberini, the bronze ceiling from the portico of the Temple of Hadrian was melted down and used to make the twisted columns of the famous baldachin (altar) in St. Peter's Basilica. This sacrifice of the "original stones" launched the Roman baroque style, much to the detriment of the immense heritage of ancient monuments. The same fate befell the Colosseum, Italy's most visited monument; it was used as a quarry, a source for stone to construct new buildings such as the Palazzo Venezia and the Palazzo della Cancelleria. Whole blocks of travertine from the Flavian amphitheater, known today as the Colosseum, were used to build the Palazzo Barberini and the port of Ripetta. However, it was Pope Julius II who, at the beginning of the 15th century, threatened the Roman Forum, the largest archaeological open-air museum in ancient Rome. On his orders, many buildings in what was once the heart of the Roman Empire, between the Palatine and the Capitoline hills, were reduced to rubble or lime dust for use in other constructions. Time did the rest, but awareness of the Forum's former splendor fascinates visitors who walk among the ruins today, or admire the many paintings of great landscape artists such as Giovanni Pannini, who inspired the "Rovinismo" movement of the 18th and 19th centuries, portraying on canvas the romantic and decadent charm of the Roman ruins and antiquities.

The vitality and regenerative power of the city's archaeological wonders is extraordinary. Take the Verona Arena, for example, one of the great symbolic sites in Italian culture. Having served as the backdrop to gladiatorial performances, it has played host, since 1913, to the world's most spectacular operatic productions, to the great delight of the 14,000 lovers of bel canto who can be accommodated in its large auditorium. The ancient theater of Taormina has undergone a similar revival; with its perfect acoustics and impressive views of Mount Etna and the coast, it has become the stunning setting for an exciting season of dance, theater, and cinema.

And in Sicily, where imposing Doric temples dominate the ancient city of Agrigento, it remains one of the Mediterranean's major archaeological sites, once described by the Greek poet Pindar as "the most beautiful of mortal cities." Here the temples themselves are the real spectacle and at sunset, illuminated by floodlights, they are revealed in all their glory, beginning with the Temple of Concord, the most important Doric building after the Parthenon in Athens to survive to this day. The temples of Paestum, another archaeological wonder of southern Italy, are almost intact. Formerly known as Poseidonia, the ancient city was founded in the 7th and 6th centuries BC *at the mouth of the River Sele, and here the charm of "original stones" combines with that of painting. The painted images on the Tomb of the Diver are the sole survivors today of paintings from the Greek age of Magna Graecia. Another depiction of a diver can be admired in what was the largest art gallery of the Etruscan epoch, the city of Tarquinia: with its painted sepulchers, it must surely have had some influence on the paintings at Paestum. The decoration on the 200 tombs in the hill of Monterozzi, the main necropolis of the Etruscan settlement, cover a time span that began with the civilization's greatest era of splendor and ended with the fall of the Roman Republic. So great is its heritage that it deserves the title of "the first chapter in the history of Italian painting." Pompeii, the most important ancient Roman open-air art gallery, must be its second chapter; magnificent wall paintings adorn almost every building in the city. Rediscovered after 17 centuries of oblivion, Pompeii owes its incredible state of preservation to the eruption of Mount Vesuvius, which buried the city and surrounding area in* AD *79. In this tragic event, time stood still at the very moment of the disaster and as a result there could be no further construction in the city, unlike in the rest of the Roman world. This is the continual "rebuilding of the monument in one's own way" to which Marguerite Yourcenar referred. However, it is to the inspiration of the brilliant archaeologist Giuseppe Fiorelli that we owe the wonderfully realistic effect that makes Pompeii such a marvel. By pouring liquid plaster into the cavities in the ash left behind by the disintegrated bodies of the city's inhabitants, he was able to produce casts that still bear vivid witness to the terrible human tragedy caused by the eruption. Fiorelli somehow anticipated the modern three-dimensional historical reconstructions that are so common today both on television and in museums throughout the world, helping us once again to relive the "original stones" of our past. However, no great special effects are needed to rediscover the most recent of the archaeological wonders of Italy: Ravenna, capital of different empires between the 5th and 6th centuries on three occasions. Owing to its early Christian and Byzantine monuments, it was registered in 1996 on UNESCO's World Heritage list. In fact, the only guide a visitor needs to Ravenn's past are its mosaics, which tell the tale of the city, a kind of Pompeii of the High Middle Ages. Whether you are in the Neonian Baptistery, the Mausoleum of Galla Placidia, or the Basilica of Sant'Apollinare Nuovo, Stendhal's words hang in the air and the spell of Italy's archaeological treasures continue to work its magic. This power can also be felt by anyone who has stood in front of the Riace bronzes over the last 40 years. These colossal bronze statues of warriors from the 5th century* BC *were recovered from the sea in Calabria in 1972 and now have their rightful place in history as some of the greatest masterpieces of Greek art.*

Arias in the Arena

VERONA

Where gladiators once fought in combat, now it is tenors who battle it out. Beneath the pink stone arches of the amphitheater, where bears and lions would wait before being let loose into the arena, today there are offices, dressing rooms, and workshops for set and costume designers for one of opera's best preserved venues: the Verona Arena. Built in the time of Augustus, the Roman amphitheater has been staging shows and events for more than 2,000 years, with an astounding playbill that has ranged from ancient Roman gladiatorial battles to medieval jousts and tournaments, from bull runs to circus spectaculars, and on to the most recent musical theater of our time. The arena is well-suited to large-scale productions, its dimensions are truly colossal. It is the third largest Roman amphitheater in world, after the Colosseum in Rome and the amphitheater of Capua, north of Naples. With its perfect acoustics and large seating capacity, the Verona Arena is the world's largest open-air opera venue, able to seat more than 14,000 spectators. But the arena today looks quite different from when it was first built outside the city walls. Of the three concentric elliptical circles that supported the stepped seating, the only one remaining is the so-called "ala," or "wing," four arches over three floors of Veronese limestone. The ala survived the terrible earthquake of 1117 that almost completely destroyed the building's facade, which must have been truly monumental. Inside there is a large auditorium containing 44 rows of terraced seating, where lovers of bel canto have been taking their places for over a century. It was, in fact, in 1913, on the hundredth anniversary of Verdi's birth, that the Verona arena's opera performances first began. *Aida*, Verdi's most spectacular and monumental work, was performed there on August 10, and from that point onward, *Aida* has been inextricably linked with the history of the theater; it has been staged there over 500 times, and could not possibly be left off the playbill for the coming centenary, when it will be staged twice: in a revival of the 1913 version, and the more radical, modern version by the Catalan group La Fura dels Baus.

234 It was the Veronese tenor Giovanni Zenatello who came up with the idea of establishing a major opera season at the Verona Arena, an annual open-air event that provides employment for 1,200 people. After Aida, the opera most often performed is Bizet's Carmen. Aida was staged at the Verona Arena for the first time on August 10, 1913, to celebrate Giuseppe Verdi's centenary. Among those who attended the performance were composers Giacomo Puccini and Pietro Mascagni, and writer Franz Kafka.

234-235 The so-called "wing," comprising 5 columns and 4 arches over 3 floors, is all that remains of the outer circles that originally formed the facade of the Verona Arena. The inner circle has a double tier of 72 arches made of white limestone from Valpolicella, forming an ellipse of approximately 148 x 243 feet (45 x 74 meters). The auditorium inside the Arena has 45 rows of marble steps.

Byzantine Splendor and Power

RAVENNA

Getting the father of analytical psychology to lie on the therapist's couch is no easy task. They know this only too well at Ravenna in Emilia-Romagna, where their magnificent mosaics set Carl Gustav Jung's imagination alight, even making him believe he saw something that wasn't there—a mosaic showing Christ extending his hand to St. Peter. That was in the 1930s, and the psychiatrist was visiting the Baptistery of Neon, one of the early Christian and Byzantine monuments that make Ravenna a UNESCO World Heritage Site. The city itself was designated a capital at three different times in the 5th and 6th centuries AD: capital of the Western Roman Empire (from 402 to 476), of the kingdom of the Goths (from 493 to 526), and lastly, of the Byzantine exarchate (from 540 to 751). The mosaics are a real testament to the power of a city that reached the pinnacle of its glory during a period known elsewhere for its decadence, at the troubled start of the Middle Ages. The most ancient of the city's mosaics are those in the Baptistery of Neon and the Mausoleum of Galla Placidia, with its impressive starry vault in the classical Roman-Hellenistic style. It is to the barbarian King Theodoric of the Ostrogoths that the city owes two of its large mosaic masterpieces, both dedicated to the cult of Arianism, the doctrine introduced to the court by the king: the Basilica of Sant'Apollinare Nuovo, with its magnificent processions of the Virgins and the Martyrs, viewed as the meeting point between Roman and barbarian styles; and the Arian Baptistery, with its representation of the baptism of Christ surrounded by the Twelve Apostles on the cupola. The Eastern influence, however, is fundamental in the decoration of the Church of San Vitale—considered Italy's most important early Christian monument—constructed not as a basilica with three naves, but with a central nucleus on an octagonal plan, topped by a frescoed cupola, with a cycle of mosaics portraying Emperor Justinian and his court. Also from the Byzantine era is the Basilica of Sant'Apollinare in Classe, constructed in the first half of the 6th century, 5 miles (8 kilometers) from the center of Ravenna, at a site originally on the Adriatic coast, although now a few miles inland in the middle of the countryside. Here, magnificent decorations on the half-cupola over the apse of the church depict St. Apollinaris surrounded by twelve sheep symbolizing the apostles of Christ.

236 *At the center of the cruciform vault of the presbytery in the Church of San Vitale, divided into four symmetrical panels, stands the Agnus Dei, the mystical Lamb of God, set against a background of 27 gold and silver stars.*

237 *The Church of San Vitale is a masterpiece of early Christian art in Italy. With a central nucleus on an octagonal plan, topped by a cupola, the principles of Eastern art are evident in the basilica.*

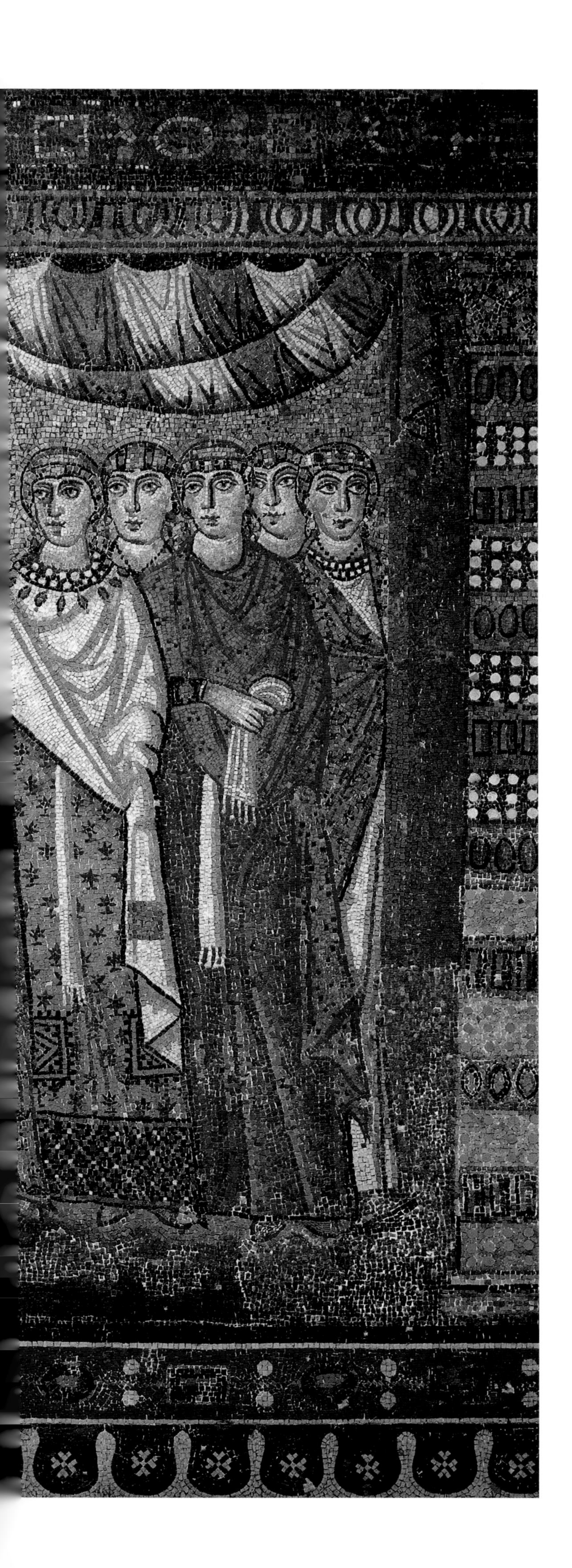

238-239 The mosaic on the south wall of the apse in San Vitale shows Theodora, wife of the Byzantine emperor Justinian, in surrounded by her entourage of seven females and two males.

239 On the north wall of the basilica is a portrait of Emperor Justinian. The processions of the royal couple depict the offering of the chalice and the paten (the bowl containing the Eucharist bread) as gifts to the church on the occasion of the consecration of San Vitale.

240-241 THE TOMB OF THE LEOPARDS, SO CALLED BECAUSE OF THE TWO BIG CATS PAINTED IN THE TYMPANUM, IS THE MOST FAMOUS OF THE UNDERGROUND TOMBS AT THE MONTEROZZI NECROPOLIS AND WAS LISTED AS A UNESCO WORLD HERITAGE SITE IN 2004.

241 THE HILL OF MONTEROZZI, THE MAIN NECROPOLIS IN TARQUINIA, OWES ITS NAME TO THE BURIAL MOUNDS, STILL VISIBLE TODAY, THAT ONCE COVERED MOST OF THE CHAMBER TOMBS EXCAVATED FROM THE ROCK.

Etruscan Tombs Bring the Dead to Life

TARQUINIA

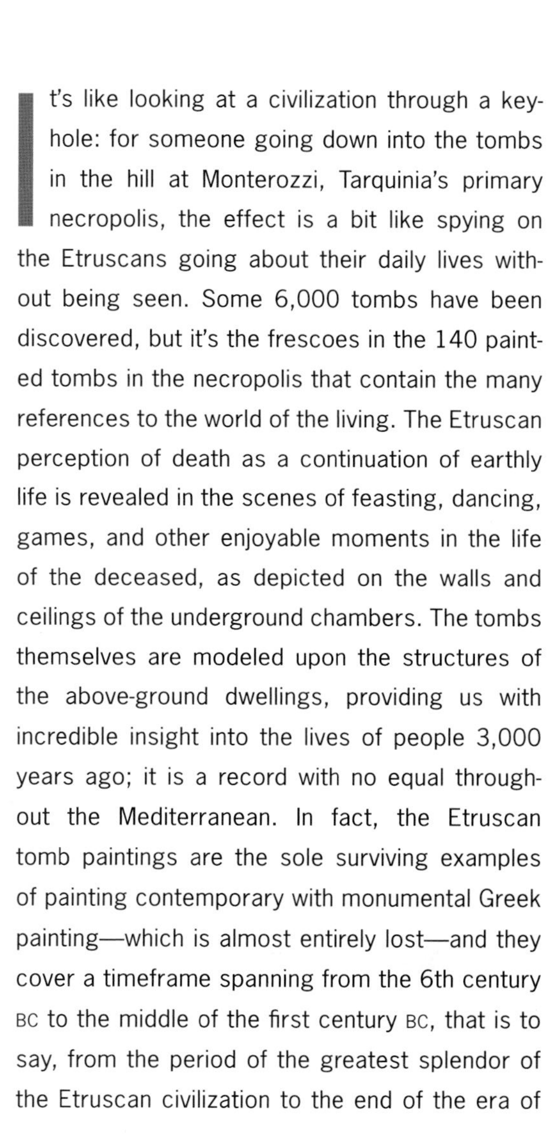

It's like looking at a civilization through a keyhole: for someone going down into the tombs in the hill at Monterozzi, Tarquinia's primary necropolis, the effect is a bit like spying on the Etruscans going about their daily lives without being seen. Some 6,000 tombs have been discovered, but it's the frescoes in the 140 painted tombs in the necropolis that contain the many references to the world of the living. The Etruscan perception of death as a continuation of earthly life is revealed in the scenes of feasting, dancing, games, and other enjoyable moments in the life of the deceased, as depicted on the walls and ceilings of the underground chambers. The tombs themselves are modeled upon the structures of the above-ground dwellings, providing us with incredible insight into the lives of people 3,000 years ago; it is a record with no equal throughout the Mediterranean. In fact, the Etruscan tomb paintings are the sole surviving examples of painting contemporary with monumental Greek painting—which is almost entirely lost—and they cover a timeframe spanning from the 6th century BC to the middle of the first century BC, that is to say, from the period of the greatest splendor of the Etruscan civilization to the end of the era of the Roman Republic. Not all of the underground chambers can be visited, but the nineteen tombs that are open to the public serve as fine examples of Etruscan funerary art. The best known is the Tomb of the Leopards (fifth century BC), which owes its name to the two big cats depicted above the frieze. The main frescoes show a banquet scene in honor of the deceased, and are striking in their particularly vivid colors of red, ocher, black, blue, and green. Also exquisite is the Tomb of Hunting and Fishing, consisting of two combined chambers, the walls of which are decorated with a seascape populated with fishes and aquatic birds, a hunter, and a diver reminiscent of the one in the fresco on the slab covering the famous Tomb of the Diver at Paestum in Campania.

242-243 IT TOOK 131,000 CUBIC YARDS (100,000 CUBIC METERS) OF TRAVERTINE STONE TO BUILD THE FLAVIAN AMPHITHEATER, BETTER KNOWN AS THE COLOSSEUM. SITUATED IN THE VALLEY BETWEEN THE PALATINE, ESQUILINE, AND CAELIAN HILLS, IT IS ALMOST 164 FEET (50 METERS) HIGH, 617 FEET (188 METERS) LONG, AND 510 FEET (156 METERS) WIDE.

243 THE COLOSSEUM HAD 80 ENTRANCE ARCHES, 76 OF WHICH WERE USED BY THE SPECTATORS, WHILE THE REMAINING FOUR, FACING THE FOUR POINTS OF THE COMPASS, WERE RESERVED FOR THE EMPEROR, OFFICIALS, AND KEY PARTICIPANTS IN THE GAMES.

The Colosseum: A History of Blood and Sand

ROME

It's been the largest and most effective PR operation of all time: for the whole world, the Flavian Amphitheater, also known as the Colosseum, begun under Vespasian and completed in AD 80 under Titus, is now inextricably linked with the power and the glory of ancient Rome. A large elliptical structure with three tiers of arcades, built on the area previously occupied by the artificial lake and gardens of Nero's Domus Aurea ("Golden House"), between the Esquiline, the Palatine, and Caelian Hills, it has managed to maintain its role throughout the centuries as a potent reminder of the past. A *sine qua non* in any view of the city, from the Middle Ages on through the Renaissance, it has been the location of choice for hundreds of films set in the capital. Just recently, the world's most famous amphitheater even "sold" exclusive image rights to Diego Della Valle, the president of the leather goods company, Tod's, for the entirely respectable figure of €25 million (US$ 33,350,000), to be used for the building's restoration (the first since 1939) and for the construction of a new service center. Putting restoration to one side, just for a moment, close your eyes and let your imagination run free, canceling out the ravages of time and imagine the Colosseum as it was when the gladiators fought there, or during the *venationes* (wild animal hunts) involving hippopotamuses, giraffes, elephants, lions, and tigers. An aura of the sacred surrounded the events that were staged there, owing to the presence of the Vestals and the emperor-god. The auditorium could seat around 50,000 spectators, divided horizontally into five sectors (*maeniana*) corresponding to social rank, although entrance was free for all. At the start of the shows, the spectators' attention would be concentrated toward the northwest and the Porta Triumphalis, one of the two monumental gates into the Colosseum. It was through this entrance that the gladiators arrived, by chariot or on foot, ready to fight in the elliptical arena, which would have been covered with sand for the occasion. But it was through the Porta Libitinensis, that the bodies of the vanquished and wounded beasts left the field. Gladiatorial combat continued until AD 404, when it was banned definitively by the emperor Honorius.

The Forum: The City's Great Stage

ROME

The great and spectacularly beautiful "engine room" of a vast empire, the Forum was situated in the valley between the Palatine and Capitoline Hills in Rome and was for centuries the heart of commercial, political, and religious life in the greatest metropolis of antiquity. It was a stage upon which "The City" (even today referred to as *Urbe*) could demonstrate its power to the rest of the world. Originating as a social and business center, following Tarquin the Proud's reclamation of the swampy land, the Forum soon grew into a neighborhood in itself, with temples, courts, churches, and markets. This forest of marble sourced from all the provinces developed alongside the Roman Empire, sharing its glory and showcasing its prosperity with new buildings, until AD 608, when the last monument, the Column of Phocas, was erected. From then on began the decline of what the Romans called the Forum Magnum, and temples and buildings eventually collapsed, becoming land for pasture. During the Renaissance, the Forum became an enormous quarry for marble and stone, and it was only in the late 1800s, after being abandoned for centuries, that it was rediscovered. Today, visitors can stroll through the Forum's ruins, framed by the Roman sky, as if through an encyclopedia of ancient history: from the Arch of Titus, constructed at the foot of the Palatine by the Senate to celebrate Titus' victories in Judea, to the Basilica of Maxentius, which appears to have been a source of inspiration for Bramante in his construction of St. Peter's Basilica. Also facing onto the Via Sacra are the Temple of Vesta, with the nearby House of the Vestal Virgins, and the Temple of Antoninus and Faustina, which has survived to the present day in excellent condition due to its conversion into the Church of San Lorenzo in Miranda. Among the best preserved buildings, past the great Basilica Emilia, where justice was administered during the Republican Era, is the Curia Iulia, rebuilt for the last time by Diocletian in AD 283. To the left of the building, erected by Julius Caesar to accommodate the Senate, behind the Campidoglio (the ancient Capitoline Hill), soar two of the most important monuments of the Forum: the triumphal arch of Septimius Severus, with 3 archways, and the 8 columns of the Temple of Saturn, at one time the seat of the Aerarium, the state treasury of Rome.

244 *The Roman Forum, the heart of political and religious life in Imperial Rome and the Republican era, stands on what once was a swampy valley, drained and reclaimed by Tarquin the Proud around the end of the 7th century.*

244-245 *From the colonnade of the Temple of Saturn, once the seat of the state treasury, there is a sweeping view of the three remaining columns of the Temple of Castor and Pollux and the Basilica of Santa Francesca Romana next to the Roman Forum.*

246 The triple Arch of Septimius Severus, built in AD 203, celebrates the emperor's victories over the Parthians. Scenes of Roman soldiers and prisoners are shown in relief on the column plinths.

247 Depicted on the north side of the Arch of Titus is the triumphal quadriga, the four-horse chariot bearing the emperor as he is crowned by Victory. The procession is preceded by the goddess Roma, who leads the horses.

The Pantheon: Where Time has Stood Still

ROME

Rome as the Romans saw it: there is only one place, beyond the ruins and the many virtual reconstructions of the Eternal City, where this is truly possible—the Pantheon. Here, everything seems to have stopped around 2,000 years ago, when the temple dedicated to all the gods was built on the orders of Emperor Hadrian, on the same site where, a century and a half earlier, another had been constructed by the consul Marcus Agrippa (later destroyed by fire). If today visitors can walk on the same marble floor as the most illustrious Roman emperors, and wander around the building's immense circular space, it is thanks to Pope Boniface IV, who, after receiving the temple as a gift from the Byzantine Emperor Phocas, transformed it into the Church of St. Mary and the Martyrs in AD 608, thereby saving it from destruction. It is not just the history of the Pantheon that has distant origins, so too have the materials used to construct it. Hadrian, a great traveler, wanted slabs of marble from Egypt for his temple, such as the pink granite used for 8 of the 16 monolithic columns making up the entry portico, which arrived in Rome from Aswan. Today the pedestal surmounting the columns is empty, but at one time it was a high-relief in bronze. The bronze from the ceiling of this portico, however, was not entirely lost. It was transformed by Bernini into the twisted columns of St. Peter's Baldachin over the high altar of St. Peter's Basilica and can still be admired today. The "theft" took place under the auspices of Pope Urban VIII Barberini, giving rise to the famous saying "What the barbarians didn't do, the Barberinis did." The interior has remained miraculously intact, with its dome—142 feet (43.45 meters) in diameter, equal to the height of the dome from the floor to the oculus (the opening at the top)—today still the world's largest unreinforced concrete dome, culminating at the top in the oculus, 30 feet (9 meters) wide, through which light filters, illuminating the entire building. Superlative architects in their achievement of the dome, the Romans had produced a roof for what Stendhal called "the most beautiful ruin from ancient Rome" by making use of a very particular kind of concrete: they mixed the cement not with gravel, but with increasingly lightweight materials as they progressed further up the dome, from travertine to the extremely light stone pumice.

248 *The oculus, the central opening in the dome of the Pantheon, is the only point through which light can enter to illuminate the building. Any rain that penetrates also drains away through 22 invisible holes in the floor.*

248-249 *The tympanum of the Pantheon is plain today, but in ancient Roman times it was decorated with a high-relief in bronze. The holes used to help secure it in place are still visible in the triangular space.*

250-251 *In the supporting walls of the Poecile, the long portico with a large rectangular basin at its center, Hadrian commissioned the building of the Hundred Chambers as servants' quarters.*

251 *The northern end of the Canopus, inspired by a canal in Egypt, was enclosed by a colonnade bearing the statues of Athena, Ares, and Hermes. Today the originals have been replaced by plaster copies.*

Villa Adriana: Hadrian's "Memoirs" Set in Stone

TIVOLI

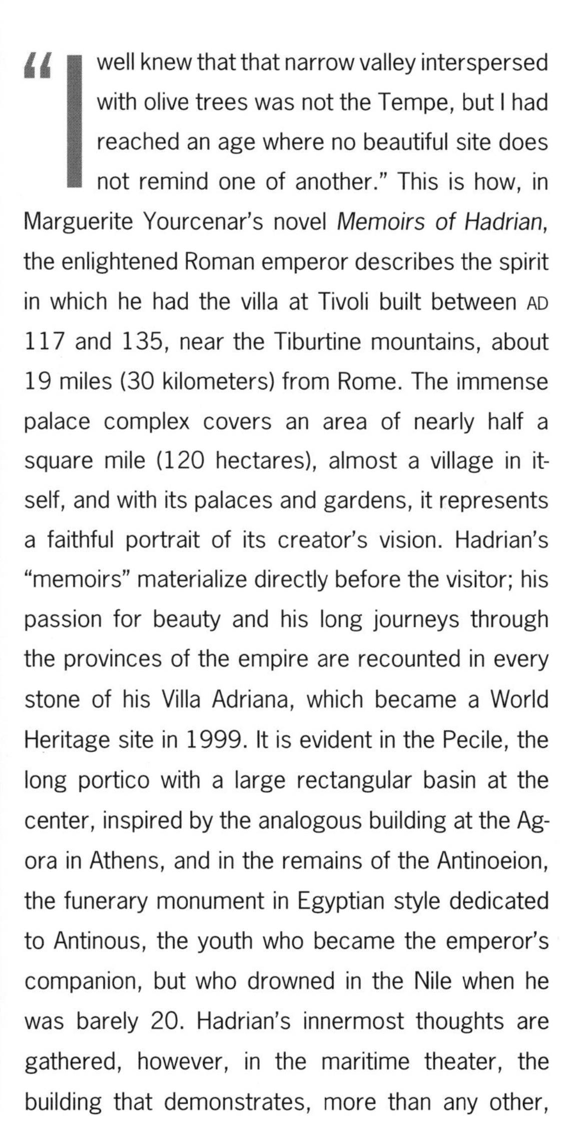

"I well knew that that narrow valley interspersed with olive trees was not the Tempe, but I had reached an age where no beautiful site does not remind one of another." This is how, in Marguerite Yourcenar's novel *Memoirs of Hadrian*, the enlightened Roman emperor describes the spirit in which he had the villa at Tivoli built between AD 117 and 135, near the Tiburtine mountains, about 19 miles (30 kilometers) from Rome. The immense palace complex covers an area of nearly half a square mile (120 hectares), almost a village in itself, and with its palaces and gardens, it represents a faithful portrait of its creator's vision. Hadrian's "memoirs" materialize directly before the visitor; his passion for beauty and his long journeys through the provinces of the empire are recounted in every stone of his Villa Adriana, which became a World Heritage site in 1999. It is evident in the Pecile, the long portico with a large rectangular basin at the center, inspired by the analogous building at the Agora in Athens, and in the remains of the Antinoeion, the funerary monument in Egyptian style dedicated to Antinous, the youth who became the emperor's companion, but who drowned in the Nile when he was barely 20. Hadrian's innermost thoughts are gathered, however, in the maritime theater, the building that demonstrates, more than any other, the villa's architectural complexity: circular in shape, surrounded by a portico supported by Ionic columns that reflect in the channel of water around the central manmade island. It is the imperial residence in miniature, where Hadrian would come to reflect in solitude. At feasts, instead, Canopus was delegated, in the form of a reproduction of the canal that connected Alexandria in Egypt to the town of Canopus, which was famous, in fact, for its banquets. Stretching 390 feet (119 meters) in length and with a width of 59 feet (18 meters), the canal terminates in a semicircular nymphaeum, and is flanked by columns and plaster casts of statues whose originals, including four caryatids copied from the Erectheion in Athens, are conserved in the nearby Antiquarium, which hosts exhibitions and permanent displays.

252-253 *The history of Pompeii began with the Opici, Italic peoples of Campania who settled in the second millennium BC on the end of an ancient lava spill on the southern slopes of Vesuvius.*

253 *The Temple of Apollo (6th century BC) is one of the oldest in Pompeii. The bronze statues, dedicated to Apollo and Diana, are reproductions of the originals now housed at the National Archaeological Museum in Naples.*

The Art Gallery of Ancient Rome

POMPEII

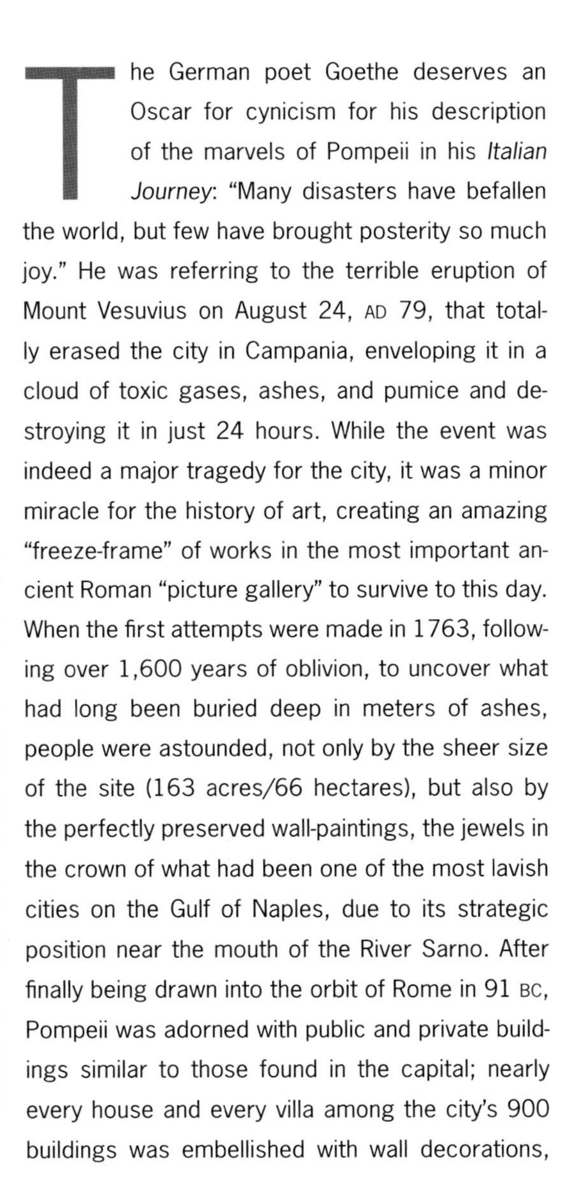

The German poet Goethe deserves an Oscar for cynicism for his description of the marvels of Pompeii in his *Italian Journey*: "Many disasters have befallen the world, but few have brought posterity so much joy." He was referring to the terrible eruption of Mount Vesuvius on August 24, AD 79, that totally erased the city in Campania, enveloping it in a cloud of toxic gases, ashes, and pumice and destroying it in just 24 hours. While the event was indeed a major tragedy for the city, it was a minor miracle for the history of art, creating an amazing "freeze-frame" of works in the most important ancient Roman "picture gallery" to survive to this day. When the first attempts were made in 1763, following over 1,600 years of oblivion, to uncover what had long been buried deep in meters of ashes, people were astounded, not only by the sheer size of the site (163 acres/66 hectares), but also by the perfectly preserved wall-paintings, the jewels in the crown of what had been one of the most lavish cities on the Gulf of Naples, due to its strategic position near the mouth of the River Sarno. After finally being drawn into the orbit of Rome in 91 BC, Pompeii was adorned with public and private buildings similar to those found in the capital; nearly every house and every villa among the city's 900 buildings was embellished with wall decorations, many of which drew upon the heritage of the great Hellenistic artists. The majority of the paintings visitors admire today when visiting the excavations, or the Museo Archeologico Nazionale ("National Archaeological Musuem") in Naples, date from the period immediately after AD 62, the year the dreadful earthquake almost destroyed Pompeii. The museum houses an important collection of frescoes, which were detached from the site and have been conserved since the time of the Bourbon kings. However, the unfortunate city's best-known paintings—the impressive megalographic frieze in the Villa dei Misteri (Villa of the Mysteries)—date from the 1st century BC. The largest group of life-sized figures to survive from antiquity, it represents the quintessential use of the emblematic color known as Pompeian red, which is synonymous with the greatest Roman art.

254-255 The House of the Vettii is one of the finest examples of the Pompeian Fourth Style, which involves architectural illusionism. The triclinium, or dining hall, housed the most famous wall paintings.

255 The House of Marcus Lucretius Fronto, who held the office of priest of Mars, reemerged following the excavations of 1895. It was a small domus from the imperial age with spectacular wall paintings in the Pompeian Third and Fourth Styles.

The Masterpiece of the Sybarites

PAESTUM

The impression created by the ruins of Paestum, which reemerged from the past when discovered in 1752, is one of prosperity, wealth, and culture. But how could it be otherwise for a *polis* founded by people whose propensity for luxury and refined pleasure was so well known that their name became synonymous with self-indulgence and high living. The Sybarites—settlers from the Achaean (Greek) colony of Sybaris, in Calabria—built a fortified settlement near the mouth of the Sele River between the 7th and 6th centuries BC. It was an ideal site, sheltered, rich with vegetation, and in a strategic position at the crossroads of trade routes. They named their city Poseidonia, in homage to the god of the sea, and to protect it, they constructed a ring of walls 3 miles (5 kilometers) long and 16 feet (5 meters) wide, which are among the best preserved from antiquity today. The perimeter, built along the edge of a limestone terrace, is pentagonal in shape, with four large gates corresponding to the cardinal points of the compass and a defensive tower on a circular base. The architectural treasures of Paestum lie inside: the three Doric temples erected in the part of the city devoted to worship. The oldest (mid-6th century BC) is also the largest; commonly known as the Basilica, it was actually dedicated to the goddess Hera. Incorrectly called the Temple of Neptune, the temple nearby (5th century BC) was also dedicated to Hera, and like the Basilica, it is peripteral in style, with columns on all sides. Beyond the forum, built after the Roman conquest on the site of the Greek agora, is the Temple of Ceres, in all likelihood dedicated to Athena, given its position in the highest part of the city. The most important discovery, now held in the Paestum Museum, dates back to the era of the three Doric temples: the painted slabs of the Tomb of the Diver, the sole example of painting from the age of Magna Graecia, the ancient Greek cities of southern Italy. In addition to the action of diving, symbolically representing the passage from life to death, the decorations depict a banquet and people traveling. In the same museum, we can also see the series of beautiful tomb frecoes from Poseidonia's Lucanian period, from 410 to 273 BC, the year the Romans conquered the city and renamed it Paestum.

256 The Temple of Ceres (500 BC), dedicated to Athena, is smaller than the other two temples at Paestum, dedicated to Hera and Poseidon. Its high pediment makes it one of the most outstanding examples of Greek architecture.

256-257 The Temple of Hera, commonly known as the Basilica, lies at the southernmost part of Paestum, next to the Temple of Poseidon, the best preserved Doric building from the age of Magna Graecia.

258 The decorations of the famous Tomb of the Diver (480 BC), discovered in 1968, are more in the Severe (early classical) style. The scene that gives its name to the grave is painted on the cover slab.

258-259 Portrayed on the long walls in the Tomb of the Diver are scenes of a banquet and a symposium, featuring people in groups of two, playing the lyre or enjoying friendly games.

Human Perfection in Bronze

REGGIO CALABRIA

At first sight of the Riace Bronzes, which depict the splendor of the male body as never before, the observer is simply overwhelmed by their beauty. Discovered at a depth of 26 feet (8 meters) by a diver from Rome, they were pulled from the waters of the Ionian Sea off the coast of Riace, in the province of Calabria, in August 1972. The immediate response to the discovery of the statues of the two Greek heroes was utter delight. The long lines that formed in 1980 in front of Florence's Archaeological Museum were unforgettable, when they were exhibited to the public for the first time after their restoration at the Opificio delle Pietre Dure (Workshop of Semiprecious Stones). The reaction aroused by the two colossal warriors from the 5th century BC far exceeded their archaeological importance. Quite apart from their being—along with the Charioteer of Delphi and the Artemision Bronze—among the precious few bronze sculptures by the great masters of the Classical Greek world that have survived to this day, the Riace warriors astonish with their lusty sensuality and sculptural perfection, enhancing the power of pectorals, biceps, shoulders, and thighs, and highlighting muscles, tendons, and veins. The realism of the casting of The Younger (Statue A) and The Elder (Statue B)—as the statues, at heights of just over 6 and a half feet (205 centimeters) and just over 6 feet (188 centimeters), respectively, have been rechristened—is enhanced by the use of subtle detailing: copper for the lips and nipples, silver for teeth and eyelashes, and ivory and limestone in the eyes. The questions still surrounding the two sculptures, which were returned to Calabria in 1982, are many, starting with their true identities and those of the artists who created them. Judging from the position of the arms, they probably represent two athletes or two warriors: each statue has one arm extended, probably to hold a lance, and the other bent, as though bearing a shield. One thing is certain, however, that the bronzes were not cast at the same time. On the basis of current scholarship, we know that The Younger dates back to 460 BC, during the Severe Period, while The Elder belongs to the Classical Period, around about 430 BC.

260 *The face of the Younger, one of the two Riace Bronzes, Greek statues discovered off the coast of Riace in 1972, has a priestly air. This bronze probably dates back to the second half of the 5th century BC.*

261 *The Elder, also known as Milziade, is in the Severe (early classical) style. It was at one time thought to be the work of the Athenian sculptor Phidias.*

262-263 The auditorium of the Greek Theater was divided vertically by 8 stairways. The steps extend from the stage to the end wall, where 8 doors opened onto a covered walkway.

263 In front of the auditorium, the stage looks out over the sea and the snowcapped peak of Mount Etna. At the rear of the stage itself are the bases for 6 columns and 4 Corinthian-style columns that were reerected in the late 19th century.

A Theater with a View

TAORMINA

The eternal "runner-up," Taormina's theater is always in second place after Syracuse, in Sicily's ranking of its classical venues. Yet apart from its size—358 feet (109 meters) in diameter compared with the 453 feet (138 meters) of its the rival—each summer Taormina's Teatro Antico is redeemed when it excels as the sparkling costar in a packed season of cinema, theater, music, and dance. The "putting on" of a show has ancient origins. The building of the theater, in fact, dates back to Hellenistic times (3rd century BC), and exploiting the natural shape of the land, the terraced seating was cut directly into the hillside. But the theater we see today on the outskirts of the historic center of Taormina town, now a favorite summer tourism destination, is bigger than the original, having been enlarged a number of times by the Romans as they were leveling the hilltop. And it is in fact the enlarged 2nd-century version of the theater, which could accommodate as many as 1,000 people, that is still welcoming spectators today. It enchants not just for its perfect acoustics, but above all for the dizzying views of Etna and of the coast that can be seen beyond the remains of the stage, capturing the greatest of Sicily's natural beauty at one fell swoop. Of the original Hellenistic theater, a few squared blocks of Taormina stone are still visible beneath the stage, and there are several inscriptions made at the time on the limestone seats. The auditorium had nine sections of terraces, crossed by eight vomitoria, the flights of access steps running between the various sectors. Behind the back wall situated at the top of the auditorium ran a double portico with a vaulted cover, over which there were two semicircular terraces with wooden seats allocated to female spectators. The third fundamental part of the ancient theater, the orchestra, a central space reserved for the choir, was transformed in the late Roman Imperial period with the removal of the first tier of steps, thus making way for the circular arena that accommodated gladiator combats and venationes, the circus spectacles with ferocious beasts that the Romans loved so much.

The Valley of Giants and Temples

AGRIGENTO

It looks just like a scene from *Gulliver's Travels*: the gigantic Telamon lies on the ground just a few paces from the Temple of Olympian Zeus. In reality, it is only a copy (the original, exhibited in an upright position, is in the Archaeological Museum of Agrigento) of one of the male statues, nearly 26 feet (8 meters) high, used to support the architrave of one of the most grandiose of all the sacred buildings in Magna Graecia, the coastal areas of southern Italy colonized by the Greeks. In the Valley of the Temples in ancient Akragas, the city founded in 582 BC by colonists from Gela, in the south of Sicily, visitors really do feel like the inhabitants of Lilliput when confronted by the impressive archaeological remains. Leaving aside the wind turbines and the construction abuses of modern Agrigento, clearly visible on the horizon from the archaeological area, it is easy to understand why Greek poet Pindar referred to this place as "the most beautiful of mortal cities." The temple ruins, visible among the agaves and olive trees, date back to the city's golden age, when it was governed by the tyrant Theron (488–472 BC), whose tomb is located outside the south wall. Of all the buildings, the best conserved is the Temple of Concordia, the most important surviving example of the Doric style temple after the Parthenon in Athens. Supported by 38 columns, it owes its excellent state of conservation to the fact that it was transformed into a Christian basilica in 597. Also on the Acropolis, in the eastern sector of the site, overlooking a cliff, is the Temple of Juno, of which 30 columns remain, and the Temple of Hercules. The oldest temple dating back to the 6th century BC, it is now reduced to a mere 8 columns that were raised in position once more around 1920. Further to the west, near the Temple of Zeus, is the temple dedicated to Castor and Pollux, sons of the king of all the gods. Only four columns remain from this temple, but they are of such beauty that they have become the symbol of the entire Valley of the Temples.

264 The Temple of Juno (5th century BC), or the Temple of Hera Lacinia for the Greeks, with 30 columns still remaining, stands overlooking the cliff and was where weddings would be celebrated in ancient times.

264-265 The Temple of Concordia was erected around 430 BC and later transformed, in AD 597, into a Christian basilica by Bishop Gregory.

266-267 The Temple of Concordia originally had white stuccoed columns and pediments painted in bright colors.

AUTHOR

FABRIZIA VILLA as a professional journalist, she has worked for over 20 years for one of the major Italian tourist magazines, writing about travel and lifestyle. After traveling through much of the world, the author is now discovering the pleasures of touring in Italy, beginning with Milan, the city she loves unconditionally and where she has always lived.

INDEX

PHOTO CREDITS

Pages 2-3 Marcello Bertinetti/Archivio White Star
Pages 4-5 Stevanzz/iStockphoto
Pages 6-7 Frank Krahmer/Corbis
Page 9 Archivio Scala, Firenze
Pages 10-11 Araldo De Luca/Archivio White Star
Pages 14-15 © De Agostini Libri S.p.A. - Area cartografia
Pages 16-17 Giulio Veggi/Archivio White Star
Pages 18-19 Araldo De Luca
Page 22 Marcello Bertinetti/Archivio White Star
Page 23 Paul Hardy/Corbis
Page 24 Elio e Stefano Ciol
Page 25 Elio e Stefano Ciol
Pages 26-27 Inge Johnsson/Age Fotostock
Page 27 Marcello Bertinetti/Archivio White Star
Page 28 Marcello Bertinetti/Archivio White Star
Pages 28-29 Marcello Bertinetti/Archivio White Star
Pages 30-31 Cameraphoto/Archivio Scala, Firenze
Page 31 Cameraphoto/Archivio Scala, Firenze
Page 33 Marcello Bertinetti/Archivio White Star
Pages 34-35 Giulio Veggi/Archivio White Star
Page 35 G. Cigolini/De Agostini Picture Library
Page 36 G. Cigolini/De Agostini Picture Library
Pages 36-37 Marcello Bertinetti/Archivio White Star
Page 38 Ghigo Roli/CuboImages
Pages 38-39 Gisella Motta/CuboImages
Pages 40-41 Matz Sjoberg/Age Fotostock
Page 41 Marco Scataglini/Marka
Pages 42-43 Antonio Attini/Archivio White Star
Page 43 Alessandro Villa/Marka
Page 44 G. Dagli Orti/De Agostini Picture Library
Page 45 Francesco del Cossa/The Bridgeman Art Library/Getty Images
Page 46 Vittorio Sciosia/Atlantide Phototravel/ Corbis
Page 47 U. Colnago/De Agostini Picture Library
Page 48 top Ivan Vdovin/Marka
Page 48 bottom Ivan Vdovin/Marka
Page 49 A. De Gregorio/De Agostini Picture Library
Pages 50-51 Antonio Attini/Archivio White Star
Page 51 Pietro Scozzari/Age Fotostock
Pages 52-53 Antonio Attini/Archivio White Star
Page 53 Antonio Attini/Archivio White Star
Pages 54-55 Joseph Sohm/Age Fotostock
Page 56 Oleg Znamenskiy/123RF
Page 57 Guido Alberto Rossi/Tips Images
Pages 58-59 Ken Kaminesky/Corbis
Page 59 top Guido Cozzi/Atlantide Phototravel/ Corbis
Page 59 bottom Gimmi/CuboImages
Pages 60-61 Giulio Veggi/Archivio White Star
Pages 62-63 Marcello Bertinetti/Archivio White Star
Page 64 Funkystock/Marka
Page 65 Sunny Celeste/Marka
Pages 66-67 Antonio Attini/Archivio White Star
Page 67 Guido Cozzi/Atlantide Phototravel
Page 68 Simone Martini/Lessing Archive/Contrasto
Page 69 A. De Gregorio/De Agostini Picture Library
Page 70 Thierry Hennet/Flickr/GettyImages
Page 71 Giulio Veggi/Archivio White Star
Page 72 G. Dagli Orti/De Agostini Picture Library
Page 73 Giuseppe Masci/Tips Images
Page 74 Frank van den Bergh/iStockphoto
Pages 74-75 José Antonio Moreno/Age Fotostock
Page 76 G. Dagli Orti/De Agostini Picture Library
Pages 76-77 De Agostini Picture Library
Page 78 Sandra Raccanello/Corbis
Pages 78-79 Antonio Attini/Archivio White Star
Page 80 G. Dagli Orti/De Agostini Picture Library
Page 81 S. Vannini/De Agostini Picture Library
Page 82 Antonio Attini/Archivio White Star
Page 83 Elio and Stefano Ciol
Pages 84-85 Archivio Scala, Firenze
Page 85 Archivio Scala, Firenze
Pages 86-87 Antonio Attini/Archivio White Star
Page 88 Wachala Jan/Age Fotostock
Page 89 Brian Jannsen/Age Fotostock
Page 90 Vito Arcomano/Marka
Pages 90-91 Marcello Bertinetti/Archivio White Star
Page 92 Marcello Bertinetti/Archivio White Star
Page 93 SGM/Marka
Pages 94-95 Alessandro Villa/Marka
Page 95 Raimund Kutter/Imageb/Marka
Page 96 Giulio Veggi/Archivio White Star
Page 97 Marcello Libra/Archivio White Star
Pages 98-99 Anne Conway/Archivio White Star
Page 99 Anne Conway/Archivio White Star
Pages 100-101 Marcello Libra/Archivio White Star
Page 101 Anne Conway/Archivio White Star
Pages 102-103 Antonio Attini/Archivio White Star
Page 103 Marcello Bertinetti/Archivio White Star
Page 104 Photoservice Electa/U/Marka
Pages 104-105 Renata Sedmakova/Shutterstock
Page 106 Antonio Attini/Archivio White Star
Page 107 Riccardo Lombardo/CuboImages
Page 110 Archivio Scala, Firenze
Page 111 Archivio Scala, Firenze
Page 112 Eightfish/The Image Bank/Getty Images
Page 113 Giulio Veggi/Archivio White Star
Page 114 G. Dagli Orti/De Agostini Picture Library
Page 115 V. Pirozzi/De Agostini Picture Library
Page 116 A. Dagli Orti/De Agostini Picture Library
Page 118-119 A. Dagli Orti/De Agostini Picture Library
Page 119 A. Dagli Orti/De Agostini Picture Library
Page 120 Archivio Scala, Firenze
Page 121 G. Nimatallah/De Agostini Picture Library
Page 123 G. Nimatallah/De Agostini Picture Library
Pages 124-125 G.Nimatallah/De Agostini Picture Library
Pages 126-127 De Agostini Picture Library
Pages 128-129 G. Cigolini/De Agostini Picture Library
Pages 130-131 Fine Art Premium/Corbis
Page 132 G.Nimatallah/De Agostini Picture Library
Pages 134-135 Collezione Dagli Orti/The Art Archive
Page 134 Araldo De Luca
Page 135 Araldo De Luca
Page 136 Araldo De Luca
Page 137 Araldo De Luca
Page 138-139 Araldo De Luca
Page 140 G. Dagli Orti/De Agostini Picture Library
Page 141 G. Nimatallah/De Agostini Picture Library
Pages 142-143 Foto Musei Vaticani/De Agostini Picture Library
Pages 144-145 Musei Vaticani
Page 146 Massimo Pizzotti/Age Fotostock
Page 147 Marco Brivio/Age Fotostock
Page 148 Archivio Scala, Firenze
Page 149 Archivio Scala, Firenze
Pages 150-151 Lessing Archive/Contrasto
Pages 152-153 Araldo De Luca
Pages 154-155 Veneranda Biblioteca Ambrosiana/ De Agostini Picture Library
Pages 156-157 F. Ferruzzi/De Agostini Picture Library
Page 158 Araldo De Luca
Page 159 Araldo De Luca
Pages 160-161 K&B News
Pages 164-165 Marcello Bertinetti/Archivio White Star
Page 165 Luciano Ramires/Archivio White Star
Pages 166-167 Luciano Ramires/Archivio White Star
Page 167 Marcello Bertinetti/Archivio White Star
Pages 168-169 Marcello Bertinetti/Archivio White Star
Pages 170-171 Marcello Bertinetti/Archivio White Star
Page 171 Giulio Veggi/Archivio White Star
Pages 172-173 Marcello Bertinetti/Archivio White Star
Page 174 S. Vannini/Corbis
Pages 174-175 Stefano Ardito
Pages 176-177 Marcello Bertinetti/Archivio White Star
Page 177 Marcello Bertinetti/Archivio White Star
Pages 178-179 U. Colnago/De Agostini Picture Library
Pages 180-181 Kreder Katja/Age Fotostock
Page 181 Antonio Attini/Archivio White Star
Pages 182-183 Antonio Attini/Archivio White Star
Page 183 G. Gnemmi/De Agostini Picture Library
Pages 184-185 Antonio Attini/Archivio White Star
Page 185 top Hermes Images/Tips Images
Page 185 bottom Antonio Attini/Archivio White Star
Pages 186-187 Antonio Attini/Archivio White Star
Page 187 Antonio Attini/Archivio White Star
Page 188 Antonio Attini/Archivio White Star
Pages 188-189 Antonio Attini/Archivio White Star
Pages 190-191 Giulio Veggi/Archivio White Star
Pages 192-193 Antonio Attini/Archivio White Star
Pages 194-195 Anne Conway/Archivio White Star
Page 195 Marcello Bertinetti/Archivio White Star
Pages 196-197 Antonio Attini/Archivio White Star
Pages 198-199 Giulio Veggi/Archivio White Star
Page 199 Westend61/Tips Images
Pages 200-201 Giulio Veggi/Archivio White Star
Page 202 Gardel Bertrand/Age Fotostock
Pages 202-203 Claudio Giovanni Colombo/ iStockphoto
Pages 204-205 Hideo Kunhara/Alamy/Milestone Media
Page 205 De Agostini Picture Library
Page 206 Marcello Bertinetti/Archivio White Star
Pages 206-207 Marcello Bertinetti/Archivio White Star
Pages 208-209 Marcello Bertinetti/Archivio White Star
Page 210 Marcello Bertinetti/Archivio White Star
Page 211 Antonio Attini/Archivio White Star
Page 212 Anne Conway/Archivio White Star
Page 213 Giulio Veggi/Archivio White Star
Page 214 top Anne Conway/Archivio White Star
Page 214 bottom Giulio Veggi/Archivio White Star
Pages 214-215 Marcello Bertinetti/Archivio White Star
Page 216 Giulio Veggi/Archivio White Star
Pages 216-217 Marcello Bertinetti/Archivio White Star
Pages 218-219 Lianem/123RF
Page 219 Alfio Garozzo/Archivio White Star
Pages 220-221 Antonio Attini/Archivio White Star
Page 222 Ludovic Maisant/Hemis/Corbis
Pages 222-223 Funkystock/Marka
Pages 224-225 Antonio Attini/Archivio White Star
Pages 226-227 Giulio Veggi/Archivio White Star
Page 228 top Giulio Veggi/Archivio White Star
Page 228 bottom Giulio Veggi/Archivio White Star
Pages 228-229 Philippe Michel/Age Fotostock
Page 230 Giulio Veggi/Archivio White Star
Pages 230-231 EasyFotostock/Age Fotostock
Page 234 Massimo Pizzotti/Marka
Pages 234-235 Antonio Attini/Archivio White Star
Page 236 A. De Gregorio/De Agostini Picture Library
Page 237 Antonio Attini/Archivio White Star
Pages 238-239 A. Dagli Orti/De Agostini Picture Library
Page 239 A. De Gregorio/De Agostini Picture Library
Pages 240-241 Alfredo Dagli Orti/The Art Archive
Page 241 Stefan Auth/Imagebrok/Age Fotostock
Pages 242-243 Marcello Bertinetti/Archivio White Star
Page 243 Marcello Bertinetti/Archivio White Star
Page 244 Giulio Veggi/Archivio White Star
Pages 244-245 Marcello Bertinetti/Archivio White Star
Page 246 Raimund Kutter/Age Fotostock
Page 247 Raimund Kutter/Age Fotostock
Page 248 Marcello Bertinetti/Archivio White Star
Pages 248-249 Marcello Bertinetti/Archivio White Star
Pages 250-251 Marcello Bertinetti/Archivio White Star
Page 251 Marcello Bertinetti/Archivio White Star
Pages 252-253 Antonio Attini/Archivio White Star
Page 253 Antonio Attini/Archivio White Star
Pages 254-255 Araldo De Luca/Archivio White
Page 255 Araldo De Luca/Archivio White
Page 256 Marcello Bertinetti/Archivio White Star
Pages 256-257 Marcello Bertinetti/Archivio White Star
Page 258 A. De Gregorio/De Agostini Picture Library
Pages 258-259 A. De Gregorio/De Agostini Picture Library
Page 260 Araldo De Luca
Page 261 Araldo De Luca
Pages 262-263 Antonio Attini/Archivio White Star
Page 263 Giulio Veggi/Archivio White Star
Page 264 Валерий Военный/iStockphoto
Pages 264-265 Antonio Attini/Archivio White Star
Pages 266-267 Alfio Garozzo/Archivio White Star

Cover :
Trevi Fountain, Rome. © Araldo De Luca

Back cover :
Detail from The Allegory of Spring by Sandro Botticelli, Galleria degli Uffizi, Florence.
© G. Nimatallah/De Agostini Picture Library

TEXTS
Fabrizia Villa

PROJECT EDITOR
Valeria Manferto De Fabianis

EDITORIAL ASSISTANT
Laura Accomazzo
Giorgio Ferrero

GRAPHIC LAYOUT
Maria Cucchi
Stefania Costanzo

METRO BOOKS
New York

An Imprint of Sterling Publishing
387 Park Avenue South
New York, NY 10016

This 2013 edition published by Metro Books,
by arrangement with Edizioni White Star s.r.l.

Translation: John Venerella
Editing: JMS Books llp

ISBN 978-1-4351-4849-9

For information about custom editions, special sales, and premium
and corporate purchases, please contact Sterling Special Sales at
800-805-5489 or specialsales@sterlingpublishing.com.

Manufactured in China

2 4 6 8 10 9 7 5 3 1

www.sterlingpublishing.com